Praise for *How to Tell People to F**k Off Politely*

A book that will help you build confidence and learn how to say no.

— La Vanguardia

A clear guide, full of practical tips.

— El Mundo

This book delivers even more than it promises.

— El Español

Praise for *How to Stop Being Your Own Worst Enemy*

This teaches the importance of managing our inner dialogue so it doesn't make our lives miserable.

— El Mundo

A book that explores how the way we talk to ourselves affects our well-being.

— Vogue España

It provides the key principles of assertiveness and self-confidence as well as mindfulness tools to silence destructive inner dialogue.

— BBVA Aprendemos juntos

HOW TO TELL PEOPLE TO F**K OFF POLITELY

ALSO BY ALBA CARDALDA

How to Stop Being Your Own Worst Enemy
(publishing July 2027)

Please visit:

Hay House USA: www.hayhouse.com®
Hay House Australia: www.hayhouse.com.au
Hay House UK: www.hayhouse.co.uk
Hay House India: www.hayhouse.co.in

HOW TO TELL PEOPLE TO F**K OFF POLITELY

The People Pleaser's Guide to Boundaries, Self-Respect, and Real Connection

ALBA CARDALDA

Translated by Ariadna Molinari Tato

HAY HOUSE LLC
Carlsbad, California • New York City
London • Sydney • New Delhi

Published in the United States by: Hay House LLC, www.hayhouse.com®
P.O. Box 5100, Carlsbad, CA, 92018-5100

Project editor: Nicolette Salamanca Young • *Translator:* Ariadna Molinari Tato
Cover design: Duró Studio and Julie Davison • *Cover illustration*: © tutu art
Interior design: Lisa Vega • *Interior illustrations:* Jorge Penny

First published in Spanish as *Cómo mandar a la mierda de forma educada* (ISBN: 978-84-19248-54-1) by Penguin Random House Grupo Editorial, S.A.U., Sant Andreu de la Barca, Barcelona © 2023 Alba Cardalda

Tradepaper ISBN: 979-8-3186-0408-9
E-book ISBN: 979-8-3186-0409-6
Audiobook ISBN: 979-8-3186-0140-2

1st Printing

Printed in the United States of America

This product uses responsibly sourced papers, including recycled materials and materials from other controlled sources.

The authorized representative in the EU for product safety and compliance is Penguin Random House Ireland, Morrison Chambers, 32 Nassau Street, Dublin D02 YH68, Ireland. https://eu-contact.penguin.ie

To Inti, who was by my side
when I was writing each of these pages.
To my family and friends for their
unconditional support.

CONTENTS

INTRODUCTION

A few years ago, I lived in a small town in Bolivia where I worked as a volunteer psychotherapist in an orphanage. Apart from acting as a therapist, I was regularly responsible for going over to the big city to buy groceries for the whole week. Once, while I was on my way to the market, my usual route was blocked due to floods caused by recent storms, and I had to take a different and unknown route. I had no map or GPS signal, so the only way I could get to my destination was by following the signs.

I had been driving under the flooding rain for about 20 minutes when I realized I hadn't seen any kind of traffic sign. No informational signs, speed limits, crossroads, stops, route confirmation signs, anything. There weren't even lines painted on the pavement. It looked more like an airport runway than a highway.

Suddenly, I saw a car coming right at me at full speed. I panicked, tensed, and held on to the wheel for dear life while I turned right and tried not to crash against the vehicle coming from the opposite direction.

We missed each other. I still don't know how.

I stopped at the curb to calm myself down while thousands of questions darted through my mind. Was I the one going in the wrong direction? Had I gotten into the wrong lane, or did the other driver invade mine? Where was my exit? How many more miles did I have to go? What was the speed limit of that highway? I was absolutely baffled.

. . .

A highway without traffic signs is very much like a relationship without boundaries: Nobody knows what they can or cannot do, what to expect from others, or whether others expect something from them. There are no simple codes distinguishing right from wrong. You can never know if you're being respectful of someone else's personal space or if they're being respectful of yours. It's unclear where someone's accountability begins and where it ends. Therefore, it's the perfect storm for accidents to happen.

Just like traffic signs help us drive safely and arrive at our destination in one piece, boundaries serve the same function in relationships: They guarantee that we relate with each other safely and that everyone's integrity is preserved.

However, we weren't taught to understand boundaries as such; we were raised to believe that setting boundaries is selfish and that true love is *always* unconditional. The ideas we were taught when we were children have become the foundation of our behavior and of our way of assimilating and interpreting relationships, and they make us blame ourselves when we set limits on the behavior of others and feel unloved when someone else sets their own boundaries. This wrongful interpretation encourages us to establish toxic, dependent, or abusive relationships, to say yes when we want to say no, and to feel unable to express our needs and emotions, even with the people we love the most.

These deeply mistaken beliefs about what boundaries are go hand in hand with a lack of emotional education and assertive communication skills. While some schools now teach courses on emotional education for toddlers and kids, most of us who were born before the turn of the century weren't given any kind of guidelines that could help us identify, name, value, and communicate our emotions in a sympathetic and assertive way. Now that we've grown up and wish to express how we feel, to say no, or to disagree, we have a hard time finding the right words. We were never taught to be simultaneously honest and respectful; we weren't taught to express our anger without attacking others, nor to eloquently share our needs with someone else.

Consequently, we usually hide what we want to say because we can't find an assertive way of doing it. We tell ourselves things like "It doesn't matter" or "I don't want to make waves" or "I don't want to upset the other person"—in other words, we self-repress. However, when we repress ourselves, instead of defusing our emotions, they grow and accumulate inside us until we erupt like a volcano and end up expressing them in the worst possible way. That's when we hurt others and our relationships.

Although we have the right to set boundaries, we must do it appropriately. Doing it while also considering both other people's emotions and our own, using adequate words, and choosing the right time to do it is key to setting healthy boundaries that help us build—rather than tear apart—our relationships with others and with ourselves. But being assertive is not enough; we also need to be familiar with effective communication strategies and nonverbal communication cues that make this hard work easier and more efficient, without undermining our relationships.

But let's start from the top.

* 1 *

BOUNDARIES—WHAT THEY ARE AND WHAT THEY ARE NOT

All of us would be transformed if we had the courage to be who we really are.

— Marguerite Yourcenar

What Boundaries Are

Boundaries are defined as a real or symbolic line that marks the end of something material or immaterial, or as a separation between two things. They establish a limit that can't or shouldn't be crossed. In psychology we talk about interpersonal boundaries, which could be defined as the lines and rules we set for our interactions that help us have healthy relationships with others and with ourselves. There are different types of boundaries, as I'll explain below.

First, we have *physical boundaries,* which have to do with personal space and physical contact. Some people enjoy physical contact and relate more intimately with others. They might touch the other person's hand or arm while they speak, they may greet others by hugging them, and they usually like physical expressions of affection. Others prefer to be more distant. They merely shake people's hands, they feel their personal space invaded when someone gets too close, and they usually find it uncomfortable if someone tries to show their love by kissing or touching them. When it comes to physical boundaries, personal preferences are as important as cultural customs and traditions. For instance, people from Northern Europe set their physical boundaries for personal proximity farther than people from Southern Europe.

Physical boundaries are also related to our private spaces, such as our bedroom, our backpack, or our pockets. Physical assaults represent the worst kind of transgression to our physical boundaries, but our boundaries are also crossed (although to a lesser extent) when someone touches us more than we enjoy, when they invade our personal space, or when they rummage through our personal belongings without permission.

Second, there are *emotional boundaries,* which have to do with how, when, where, and to whom we choose to express our emotions. These are crossed if someone emotionally blackmails us or if they disregard our emotions or judge us for saying how we feel. Our emotional boundaries are also violated when someone meddles in our emotional interactions (for instance, if they hear our conversations or read our messages or mail) or when they go through places where we have shared our feelings and thoughts (like our personal diary) without asking us for permission.

Another kind of boundaries are *sexual boundaries.* These have to do with the emotional, communicational, and physical aspects involved in sexual relationships. They are not only transgressed through nonconsensual physical or sexual contact but also through inappropriate sexual comments or gestures and any form of coercion that leads to unwanted sexual contact.

Temporal boundaries have to do with how much time we choose to devote to our different activities and to the people around us. When someone demands that we spend more time than we desire with them or more than the time we previously set apart for a certain activity (such as our working hours, for instance), they are violating our temporal boundaries.

Finally, *material boundaries* are those related to the private property of objects or commodities. They have to do with what we choose to do with our possessions or with whether we want to share them and with whom. When someone steals something from us, borrows something without permission, damages it without intending to replace it, or pushes us to use our belongings in a certain way, they are trespassing on our material boundaries.

. . .

Some types of interpersonal boundaries are harder to identify and set than others. It's not as difficult to establish the most tangible boundaries, such as material or physical ones, as it is to establish those we can't see, such as emotional boundaries. That is why everyone knows that they shouldn't grab someone else's car keys and take their car without permission, but not everyone understands as clearly that no one should feel entitled to manipulate our feelings and force us to do what they want.

Similarly, it's easier to set quantifiable boundaries—such as temporal boundaries—than nonquantifiable ones—such as sexual boundaries. We feel completely entitled to act upset if someone arrives one hour later than agreed, but we don't feel it's equally valid to express our discomfort when someone gives us a lewd look.

The beliefs ingrained in our culture and taught at school also influence each type of boundary differently. For instance, if we're physically assaulted, we have no doubt whatsoever that we have the right to defend ourselves without feeling guilty about it. However, if someone hurts our feelings and our psychological integrity, we are overcome by guilt if we ask that person to change their behavior.

Why does this happen? Aren't we trying to protect ourselves from harm in both cases?

The first task we face when we want to establish boundaries for the first time is to deem both as equally important.

For instance: You would never dream of removing the front door of your house and giving unlimited access to anyone and everyone, right? You would run the risk of being mugged or harmed, and it would jeopardize the safety of your family. That is why everyone has a front door at home that can be opened only with a key owned by its inhabitants. If anyone else wants to come in, they must ring the bell, and it's your choice whether to let them in or not. Similarly, inside your house there are other doors that separate bedrooms and other private and shared spaces. Nobody finds it offensive if every family member has their own personal space at home and keeps the door open or closed as they wish. Nobody minds if someone else closes the bathroom door when they're using it, nor do we feel guilty when we're the ones closing it from inside. We accept these boundaries as normal and necessary for harmoniously coexisting.

How would you react if a friend got upset because you haven't given them a key to your house? What would you say if they argued that they should be able to come and go as they please if you really loved them? What would you do if they claimed that not giving them a key to your house means that you don't trust them or love them at all?

You would probably think they're being irrational, and unless they seem to be experiencing an actual psychotic breakdown or something similar, you would probably end that relationship as soon as possible.

When someone disrespects any kind of boundary we set and expect our love for them to be unconditional, or when they dislike that we say no to them or become upset when we express our emotional need, they are being as disrespectful and shameless as the "friend" who wants to have a key to our house. We should never give in to that kind of blackmail, no matter how much we care for that person.

Boundaries are an act of love for others, despite what we've been led to believe. When you clearly express what you want and need from a relationship, you're making things easier for the other person: Now they know how to make you feel comfortable and safe, and you can have a healthy and long-lasting relationship with them. It's like saying, "Since I love you and I want us to have a long and sweet relationship, I want to share with you the things that make me feel good, so you don't have to guess them or end up unintentionally hurting me and driving a wedge between us." Similarly, becoming interested in the other person's boundaries shows how much you want to invest in having the healthiest possible relationship with them while making them feel safe. Boundaries are also an act of self-love, because by setting them, you listen to your own needs and honor them, while giving yourself exactly what you need and nothing else when you relate to other people.

Setting boundaries implies that you respect other people, on the one hand, because it's like telling them, "While I'm sharing my boundaries with you and expect you to respect them, I hope you also share yours with me, and I'll respect them." On the other hand, it's an act of self-respect because, when you value your own rights and needs, and you try to have others respect them, you're honoring yourself as a human being.

Boundaries imply that you accept the other person as they are because you acknowledge that whatever they would allow in a relationship may be very different from what you would allow, and that doesn't make their boundaries any less valid. Setting boundaries is an act of self-acceptance because it implies the acknowledgment and validation of our own needs and wishes without judging ourselves or feeling guilty about it.

• • •

It's impossible to understand what boundaries are without discussing our basic assertive rights. These are rights we all have simply because we are human beings, and they are meant to safeguard our needs and everyone else's by establishing where everyone's personal freedom begins and ends. Not only do they help establish respect and ethical and moral codes, but they also justify interpersonal boundaries that we set upon ourselves and others. The basic assertive rights are:

- the right to express feelings, emotions, thoughts, and needs
- the right to be treated with respect and dignity
- the right to disagree
- the right to say no
- the right to want something
- the right to not want something
- the right to change your mind
- the right to make mistakes
- the right to decide on your own life, body, and time
- the right to establish your own priorities

However, having rights inevitably means we also have responsibilities. In this case, these 10 basic rights entail only one responsibility: to respect everyone else's assertive rights.

Children also have the same rights—except for the last two—as long as their decisions do not compromise their integrity or the integrity of others. Respecting these rights during childhood is essential because that's when children develop their beliefs about themselves and about others and the world. If someone makes you feel like you don't have any of these rights when you're growing up, by the time you reach adulthood, you'll find it hard to believe that you have them and consequently defend them. If you deprive a child of their basic assertive rights, you condemn them to be easily manipulable and vulnerable to abuses, since they won't feel they have the right to express their feelings, to say no, to communicate their needs, or to make their own decisions. That's why it's vital to respect children's assertive rights, because they will learn from us how to exert and defend them.

One way in which humans learn is by imitating. Children learn information and habits by imitating their older siblings, their classmates, their cartoon superheroes, and, especially, their parents. That is why parents should not only respect their child's assertive rights but also teach them by example how to defend one's own rights and respect others'. It's pointless to tell a child what to do if we don't talk the talk and walk the walk.

What Boundaries Are Not

Boundaries are not telling someone what they should or shouldn't do. Setting them is not the same as demanding something or forbidding someone from doing something but rather expressing what we need from that relationship and what makes us feel good. Having the right to express our needs doesn't mean we can do it however we want or without considering the other person's feelings. We shouldn't confuse our freedom of speech with saying whatever we want however we want; your freedom ends where the other person's rights begin. For instance, saying, "I want you to text me when you get home" is not a boundary. In this case, you're imposing an obligation on the other person without respecting their right to decide if they want to do it or not. But we can communicate our wishes or needs by saying, "I would appreciate it if you texted me when you got home; otherwise, I get worried." Then the other person can honestly express whether they agree to do it or not.

Boundaries are not up for judgment. You cannot choose what you want or what you need. It's just how you feel! Therefore, you shouldn't judge your own boundaries. Likewise, we shouldn't judge other people's boundaries. We can only accept them and honor them, or, if they're incompatible with ours, we can decide whether we want to keep that relationship or not.

This last part is a bit more controversial than it seems at first, since some wishes and needs are not actually healthy because they are based on limiting beliefs or personal insecurities, and they hurt both us and our relationships. For instance, if you feel the overwhelming need to control everything, it will probably end up hurting you and the people you interact with. If that is the case, instead of judging what you need, try questioning it: *Why do I feel the need to control things? Is it good or bad for me? How does it influence my relationships? How does it affect the people I love? Does it have to do with an insecurity of mine?* When you observe it without judging it, you can work on improving that part of yourself.

Finally, boundaries are not a synonym of selfishness. Setting boundaries is not a selfish act; on the contrary, boundaries are intended to help relationships work as adequately as possible, which can happen only if the people involved feel comfortable and free to give their very best.

When we learn what boundaries are and what they are not, we begin to see them as tools for strengthening our relationships (both with others and with ourselves) in ways that support each person's dignity—and recognize that setting boundaries is an essential building block of healthy love.

* 2 *

RELATIONSHIPS, HEALTH, AND HAPPINESS

A good life is built on good relationships.

— Robert Waldinger

A Revealing Study

Throughout history, from Aristotle's day to ours, great thinkers, philosophers, psychologists, anthropologists, scientists, and other illustrious minds have been interested in understanding happiness and its causes. What makes some people feel happier than others? Is it possible to breed happiness? What influences our perception of happiness? Are we born happy, or do we make ourselves happy? For a few centuries, human beings have asked themselves infinite questions about happiness without finding particularly compelling answers. *Until now.* Researchers at Harvard University have been carrying out one of the longest and most extraordinary longitudinal studies ever done on happiness. For over 85 years, the Harvard Study of Adult Development has followed an initial group of 724 people to determine what makes them happy. Participants come from different socioeconomic backgrounds and have participated from their adolescence to adulthood. Researchers collected data through the years about participants' professional, family, and sex lives, as well as their habits, health, and finances, among other things.

As the years passed, the study was expanded to include not only the original participants but also their children and partners, resulting in thousands of pages of gathered data—and its analysis revealed something stunning. Dr. Robert Waldinger, current director of the study, claims that the results are quite clear: Happiness has nothing to do with social status, academic degrees, the place we live in, or the food we eat. Instead, the key to a happy and healthy life is the quality of our close relationships. This conclusion was surprising because, for the first time, it was scientifically proven that the key to our happiness lies in how we relate to others. And not only that, but it was also proven how much relationships influence our health.

George Vaillant, the psychiatrist who led the study between 1976 and 2004, published a book about the factors that influence our health the most when we grow old. Vaillant explains in *Aging Well* how genetics, physical exercise, food, and alcohol and drug abuse affect us. His final thesis was very compelling: "The key to healthy aging is relationships, relationships, relationships."

Finding out that relationships have such a pivotal impact on our health and our longevity was one of the most amazing findings of this study. Researchers proved that, for instance, people in their fifties with good healthy relationships were healthier by the time they reached their eighties, and that elderly people with safe relationships experienced less cognitive and physical decline and had a better long-term memory when compared to people without them. On the other hand, they also observed that good relationships have a positive impact on a person's sleep quality and ability to handle stress, which makes them an essential factor for preventing several serious diseases.

Plenty of other studies from different disciplines have supported these findings and have marked a turning point in how we understand and handle our physical, psychic, and emotional health.

A Work of Art

There are astonishing works of art that can reach through your eyes to touch your soul. There are songs that can dissolve the biggest lump in your throat and give you goosebumps with just their first three chords. But there is one thing so amazingly extraordinary that allows for the existence of all the other works of art that make the world make sense: the brain.

Research on the workings of the brain is amazing. It has shown how each area, each structure, each cell, and each atomic particle that is part of a brain cell performs a specific role. And that's what makes nature so remarkable.

When you get excited about a song, when a specific smell brings you back to a childhood memory, when you fall in love, when you read a novel, when you learn something new, when you get out of bed, or when you make yourself coffee. . . . Every single thing you do throughout your life, no matter how big or small, and every feeling or thought you have is possible thanks to specialized brain cells that process specific kinds of information.

For instance, imagine you're having dinner with your family and someone sitting on the other side of the table suddenly calls out to you: "There it goes! Catch it!" Then, they throw something in the air. During the few seconds it takes the object to go from one side of the table to the other, billions of cells activate in certain areas of your brain specialized in perceiving, analyzing, and reacting to what is about to happen, without you even being aware of it.

There are some cells in the brain, located in the occipital lobe (the back of your head), that are part of the visual system. Within this system, some specific brain cells analyze the surface of an object; others detect its color; others, its shape; others, its size; others, its speed; others, the direction it is taking. And thus, in less than a second, these specialized groups of brain cells send the information to another specific group of brain cells that assimilate it. Your semantic memory—the mental encyclopedia where you keep all the data about the objects with which you're familiar—activates right away, and the information from the visual system is integrated with the word from your encyclopedia that fits best. Then, your brain determines that the object coming at you is an orange. It's not an apple or a tennis ball; it's an orange.

Additionally, while all that information is being processed, the prefrontal lobe enacts the decision to make you move so you can dodge the object. It tells the brain cells in charge of moving the upper part of the body that the core, arms, and head muscles should move to a side so that the orange won't hit you directly in the face. Simultaneously, a different part of the brain—which controls reflexes—makes you close your eyes to protect them from the possible impact. But that's not all: In the meantime, billions of other brain

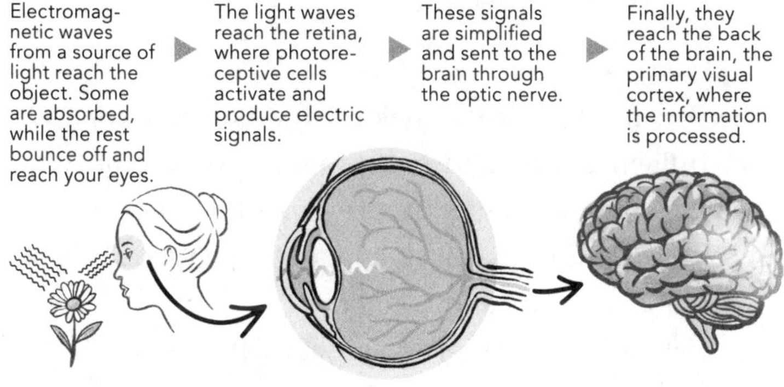

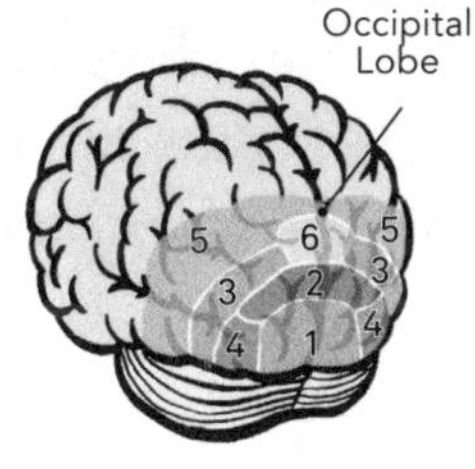

The occipital lobe, the visual processing area of the brain, deciphers all the following visual information:

1. General exploration
2. Stereoscopic vision
3. Depth and distance
4. Color
5. Movement
6. Absolute position of the object

cells remain active to help you breathe, pump blood, maintain your muscle tone, control your bladder and bowels, blink, digest food. . . . If you also yell, "What the hell are you doing?!" while you dodge the orange, your complex speech system also activates, and other sets of brain cells exchange information and allow you to speak up. That's how fascinating and complex the functioning of the brain is!

As I said earlier, all of this happens automatically in less than a second, and it constitutes one of the most basic brain functions. Therefore, it becomes difficult to imagine the intricacies of the mechanisms for harder activities, such as writing, playing an instrument, planning your vacations, or solving a math problem.

. . .

When it comes to neuropsychologic studies on how relationships influence our health and our subjective perception of happiness, some neuroscientists have gone a few steps further and explored the mechanisms responsible for this to help us understand how they affect our brain.

You probably know for a fact that when someone treats you with hostility, you experience negative sensation; in contrast, if someone treats you nicely, you experience pleasant sensations. These sensations are what we call feelings, and they're produced by the brain's limbic system (the main structure involved in processing emotions) in response to certain stimuli (in this case, someone's words or behaviors).

What makes emotions nice/pleasant or unpleasant/painful is the type of hormone or neurotransmitter your brain produces in reaction to those stimuli. If someone is hostile to you, your neurotransmitters and hormones experience a series of changes that produce unpleasant emotional sensations; if, on the contrary, a person treats you nicely, a different set of chemical changes take place in your brain that produce pleasant emotions.

When your body constantly produces cortisol, this substance becomes a powerful health risk factor, since it can cause heart disease, high blood pressure, strokes, lipid metabolism disorders, gut issues, loss of memory, lack of concentration, anxiety, and depression. Consequently, being surrounded by people who treat you badly is a health risk factor. The findings from these studies are not irrelevant at all, since

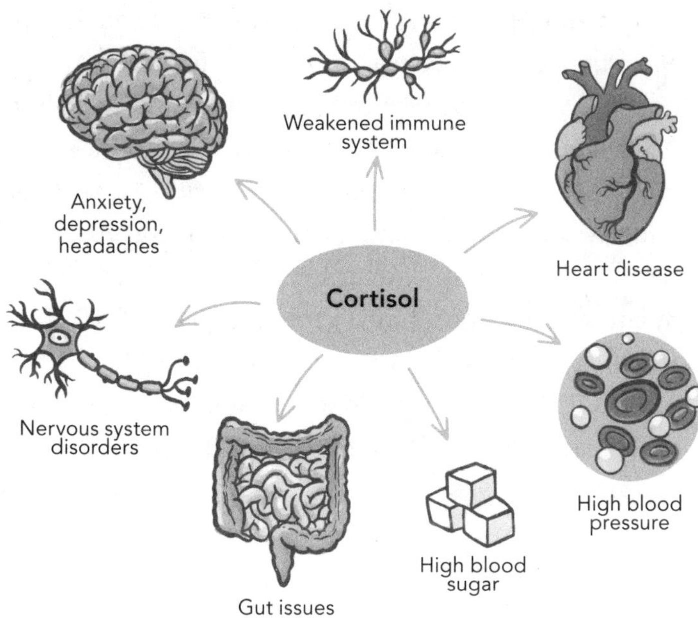

we've spent years trying to find the key to a healthy life (a balanced diet, physical activity, refraining from consuming alcohol or drugs, etc.) while completely overlooking the effect that hostile relationships have on us—which is, in fact, one of the most decisive factors.

Knowing what science has observed about the impact of personal relationships on our health compels us to reconsider our relationships as meticulously as we should. But it's inevitable to start asking more and more questions, which leads to a huge entanglement of queries:

What does a healthy relationship look like? Can a relationship be healthy and painful at the same time? Can a toxic relationship make me happy? What makes a quality relationship? How can I improve my existing relationships? What should I do about relationships that harm me? Are conflicts indicative of bad relationships? Is it possible to "reform" a toxic relationship and make it healthy? Where's the middle ground between setting boundaries and being flexible so that I can have healthy interactions? How do relationships affect the way in which we communicate? Is it possible to express my annoyance without hurting the other person? How much hostility can a person sustain before becoming ill?

This list of questions is long and complex, but I'll try to answer each one of them in the following chapters.

* 3 *

QUALITY RELATIONSHIPS

What is essential is invisible to the eye.

— ANTOINE DE SAINT-EXUPÉRY

Quality Products Versus Quality Relationships

Remember the last time you bought a new phone, a new pair of shoes, or a good bottle of wine? You probably compared a few options before finally choosing one.

When you have to choose between different options (leaving aside aesthetic or design aspects), your brain takes into consideration these three specific factors:

1. the need you want to meet
2. the quality of the product that is able to meet it
3. the price you're willing to pay for it

This assessment takes place in your brain automatically. Try to observe how your brain answers the following questions really quickly:

1. Would you pay the same for an old phone as you would its latest version?

2. Would you buy shower slippers for running?
3. If you're preparing a sangria, would you use the same wine you drank on your last wedding anniversary?

Each of these questions made you consider your answer in terms of the price of the product, your specific needs, and the quality of the product, and it's quite likely you replied to them in less than a second. That's because in your prefrontal lobe, there are brain cells specialized in making decisions that are in charge of automatically considering these three factors without you being really aware of it. This happens because you know very well the characteristics a product should have to be considered a quality product and the importance of getting value for your money that helps you make decisions quite quickly.

However, when it comes to the quality of our relationships, which is much more relevant and influential in our lives than the quality of material things, we don't have much clue of what it means. We live in a society where people pay more attention to the quality of the things they buy than to the quality of their relationships because they tend to value material possessions more than the people around them.

This is because the consumer society has taught us to believe that consuming more and obtaining things that are better than the ones we already have will make us happy, and to completely take for granted what is truly valuable. Nobody has said it better than Antoine de Saint-Exupéry when writing about the relevance of personal relationships in *The Little Prince:* "What is essential is invisible to the eye." However, we spend our whole lives chasing the unattainable carrot, believing that having a better smart phone will make us happy. However, once we have the newest phone in our pocket, we realize that the happiness we yearn for is nowhere to be found. Then we convince ourselves that we need to buy a better car, but once it's inside the garage, we realize we're still equally happy or unhappy as before. Therefore, we acquire a second home for the holiday seasons, but once we start enjoying it, we realize we feel exactly the same as before. . . . And it goes on and on with every single thing we buy. We sustain the belief that happiness lies outside us and that it depends on us buying the best, the biggest, the most expensive things. But that couldn't be further from the truth.

The Marketing Industry

Try to imagine that, instead of making you believe that buying a product would make you happy, the advertisements you have seen your entire life had told you that happiness lies in the quality of your personal relationships. If that had been the case, ever since you were a child, you would have adequately valued the way in which you relate to your family and friends, and how they relate to you. You wouldn't have let anyone treat you badly, nor would you have treated others badly; you wouldn't have sustained relationships in which you didn't feel respected, and you would have made sure you treated others respectfully. You wouldn't have allowed others to take advantage of you, and you would have tried to be more reciprocal to others based on how they treated you. You would have honored your wants and needs better, and you would have understood that other people have their own wants and needs; you would have known that they may not be the same as yours, but that doesn't make them bad people. Finally, you would have developed better skills for assertive communication and more strategies to face rejection without feeling scorned, which would help you maintain more quality relationships.

Unfortunately, the actual society we have built is based on the consumption of goods and services, not on relationships or care. Although it's a bit pointless to lament it, we can certainly reflect on it to make better decisions from now on that help improve our future.

What Is a Quality Relationship?

If you want a better future in which you're able to prioritize your personal relationships, the first thing you must understand is what a quality relationship is.

Quality relationships are those in which the people involved feel free to express their wants, needs, and limits without feeling judged, and where one of the parties can freely decide whether they want to accept the other's wants, needs, and limits. In quality relationships there is no space for manipulation, either conscious or unconscious, and the parties involved know how to treat each other because they feel free to ask for and communicate respectfully and lovingly what they require and what they dislike. It's the kind of relationship where conflicts are neither destructive nor invalidating, and where they do not compromise mutual support; it's a relationship where forgiveness, gratitude, and love are expressed through sincere words and actions.

These are essential conditions for having a quality relationship, which doesn't mean that the parties involved can't also consider other conditions necessary, based on their own values. Everyone has their own unique and personal way of experiencing relationships. Each of us gets to decide what is essential and what is not, based on the foundations of healthy relationships, our own standards, and the characteristics of our relationships.

A very helpful exercise for evaluating more accurately whether or not you have quality relationships is to closely analyze how you relate to the most significant people in your life and rate from 1 to 10 how many of the essential conditions for quality relationships are present in each one and to what extent.

I have included the following chart that you can use as a guide, along with example ratings for the "mom" column.

Rating relationships from 1 to 10 is an entirely subjective exercise with no right or wrong answers, because they depend on how you perceive each of these aspects. By analyzing them like this, you turn abstract aspects of your relationship into

	My relationship with . . .				
Relationships have a good quality when . . .	Parent 1	Parent 2	Partner	Friend 1	Friend 2
▶ . . . the parties involved feel they can express their wants, needs, and limits without feeling judged.					
▶ . . . the parties involved can freely decide whether they want or can accept the other person's limits and act accordingly.					
▶ . . . communication is based on respecting each other, without invalidating the other person's opinions or imposing one's opinions.					
▶ . . . none of the parties involved exerts any form of manipulation, regardless of whether it's conscious or unconscious.					
▶ . . . the parties involved know how to treat each other because they feel free to assertively ask for and communicate what they need and what they dislike.					
▶ . . . any conflict that arises is not destructive or invalidating, and it does not compromise the mutual support between the parties involved.					
▶ . . . forgiveness, gratitude, and love are expressed either explicitly or implicitly, with honest words or actions.					

precise and manageable ones, allowing you to identify where there are difficulties and know where to act, instead of just prodding about in the dark.

Interpreting the results also depends on what you consider to be acceptable. However, keep in mind that aspiring to a 10 (either in your relationships or in any other part of your life) is an ideal rather than a realistic objective. If you become obsessed with perfection, you'll most likely feel frustrated on a regular basis and fail to enjoy the positive results, leaving you permanently unsatisfied.

A more realistic and healthy perspective for us is to accept that giving a 7 to any aspect in our life is quite positive, an 8 is great, and anything above that is basically a miracle. Therefore, if we follow these parameters, we can clearly observe whether we have quality relationships or not, and which specific aspects of our relationships we should be working on to improve them.

Finally, if you want to make the most of this exercise, you can ask yourself questions about the aspects with lower rates in order to obtain useful information that helps you improve that specific part of your relationship. For instance, if in your relationship with a family member you have rated the first condition with a 3, you might want to ask yourself, "Why did I choose a 3 and not a 7? What would need to happen for me to rate it with a 7? Am I the one feeling judged, or am I judging the other person? When does this happen? How does it happen? If I'm the one feeling judged, is it because the other person misbehaved, or is it the result of one of my emotional wounds?" This exercise will give you enough information to take appropriate measures and begin working on either the weak points of your relationships or your own.

* **4** *

THE THREE BUILDING BLOCKS—CULTURE, BELIEFS, UPBRINGINGS

One child, one teacher, one pen, and one book can change the world. Education is the only solution.

– Malala Yousafzai

A Model of the World

A person may have all kinds of reasons for choosing to see a therapist: childhood trauma, low self-esteem, couple problems, mood disorders, mental disorders, grief, inner conflicts. . . . Regardless of what brought them there, the way in which someone relates to the people closest to them (their partner, family, friends, boss, or colleagues) and to their own self is always influenced by these issues. Therefore, one of the most important things that we deal with in therapy is the kind of relationship the individual has (or had in their childhood) with the people around them: In other words, the quality of the relationships and the communication style that characterizes them, as framed by their own model of the world.

Everyone has their own unique model of the world, different from everyone else's, which is made up of "mental filters" that make us see and interpret reality in a very specific way. These mental filters are constituted by our own personal experiences, beliefs, and values; our context, education, and culture; and our expectations, personality, and mood. This is why there are as many interpretations of a single thing as there are people perceiving it.

Once we understand that each of us has our own mental map of the world, defined by our own filters, we can become more tolerant and capable of building healthy and respectful relationships.

When we discuss a client's relationships in therapy, these should always be framed by the client's model of the world, and we should observe them from that point of view so we can grant them real meaning and identify aspects that may become maladaptive in each case. This analysis brings forward the difficulties to set boundaries: Some people are unable to identify their own boundaries or feel unable to set them; others don't know how to express them; some people may prioritize the other's boundaries, needs, and wants before their own, perhaps because of their lack of self-esteem or due to certain beliefs; and some people only uphold their own boundaries without respecting others'.

Culture

Although scientists and mental health specialists have repeatedly shown how much the quality of our relationships influences our physical and emotional health, we're still waiting for schools, universities, companies, and senior centers to incorporate this subject into their curricula and agendas. Institutions insist on prioritizing productivity and academic intelligence, even though these things don't help us feel better about ourselves or understand our emotions (but they do help support the status quo). Thus, we ignore our emotional intelligence, which is the only type of intelligence that can encourage the creation and maintenance of quality relationships with others and with oneself.

Although in recent years there has been a significant increase in cases of depression, anxiety, and other mental disorders, as well as in global suicide rates, no political party is lobbying for initiatives to promote our emotional intelligence nor to include the subject of relationships in educational syllabi. If we had been taught in school how to establish healthy relationships with others and with ourselves, to respect our own rights and the rights of others, to efficiently express how we feel or think, to set boundaries, to say no without feeling guilt, or receiving no for an answer without feeling offended, just like they taught us math or language, our lives would be completely different. However, as I've said before, our society and our culture have not prioritized the quality of personal relationships, which is why the main socializing agents (such as media, school, and families, who are responsible for passing on norms, values, and behavioral models) contribute to our stress rather than to our well-being.

Many people—especially those born before the turn of the century, and most notably women—have been indoctrinated to choose the opposite of self-care. We're taught to be kind and servile, even if that requires us to do something we don't want to do. We believe that we should fulfill the needs of others in order to be loved, even if that requires us to deny our own needs. We're told that our value relies on society approving our behavior and appearance, even if that requires us to betray ourselves and risk our health. To be a good mother, father, wife, husband, daughter, son, friend, partner, or citizen, we must never, ever say no, because doing so might make others feel bad or, even worse, make *us* undeserving of love.

As you can see, our modern culture represents one of the main obstacles when it comes to learning how to set boundaries assertively and guiltlessly.

Beliefs

When people receive these messages not only from society but also from their family and educators, they gradually form four main limiting and damaging beliefs:

1. The way others feel is more important than how you feel.
2. Thinking about your own well-being makes you bad or selfish.
3. Saying no to a request makes you unworthy of love.
4. Real love is unconditional.

In many cases, these beliefs make children grow up to become people pleasers and lead them to self-abandonment and self-neglect, which has terribly negative effects on their self-esteem.

These are submissive people, characterized by the following traits:

1. finding it very difficult to set boundaries and command respect
2. taking other people's boundaries personally
3. saying yes when they would rather say no, and agreeing to doing favors or participating in plans they would rather avoid
4. interpreting every no they receive as a personal form of rejection
5. maintaining toxic relationships and tolerating abuses at work, in social circumstances, or from family members
6. having a hard time saying how they really feel or what they really think because they prefer not to make waves
7. feeling the need to be liked and validated by everyone
8. feeling anxious, angry, or sad about many social situations
9. having low self-esteem due to their own self-neglect
10. having existential crises, believing they have not fulfilled their purpose or dared to live the life they wanted

Although submissive people may be aware that they are in deeply abusive relationships, they're afraid of saying "Stop! No more! I've had enough!" They were instilled with plenty of beliefs about what they should do for others, leaving aside and invalidating what they needed or felt. These limiting beliefs keep them at the mercy of other people's wants and needs, which is why they end up neglecting their own needs, leaving themselves until last and annulling their own purposes and vital goals. They even hesitate to speak for themselves, command respect, defend their rights, or vindicate their human dignity in the face of cruel and disrespectful abuses against them.

These people need to learn to say no and "enough is enough." They need to *re-dignify* themselves—to urgently get hold of their dignity and defend it.

Not everyone who has a hard time setting boundaries is submissive. However, most of us were taught we should please others, and we all hold beliefs to some extent that make us feel guilty when we say no or express our boundaries. Therefore, we need to redefine our boundaries and learn how to reframe them. We must feel we deserve respect, reclaim it without fear or hesitation when we are disrespected, and take appropriate actions when our rights are violated. In the same vein, we must also learn to respect others' needs and accept their boundaries without taking them as a personal attack.

You must deconstruct these deeply rooted beliefs if you want to understand why saying yes doesn't make you a better person and why saying no is not an act of selfishness. Loving doesn't mean accepting everything unconditionally, devoting yourself limitlessly to someone else, or giving up on your personal projects. It is possible to love—and to love deeply, for that matter—from a healthier and less painful place where there is also space to take care of and look after yourself, and to respect and love yourself freely, without feeling guilty or selfish about it. To do so, you must begin by questioning three key elements you learned growing up that determine how you build your relationships with others: your self-esteem, your conception of selfishness, and your idea of love.

Upbringings

Your understanding of self-esteem and selfishness depends on what you were taught love was—both for yourself and for others—when you were growing up.

Some of the circumstances that may have led you to believe that loving yourself was selfish are:

Your Role Model Was a People Pleaser

If, for example, your mother did everything for her children and her husband; prepared in advance so things were always ready when needed; stayed up until very late to finish cooking, ironing, and cleaning the house; and never said no when a neighbor asked for a favor, even if she didn't have any time left to look after herself or to get some rest, you may have learned that this was an appropriate social behavior and that spending time on yourself was wrong.

If this was your model, you'll probably follow a similar pattern, and it may be difficult to teach yourself that taking time off for joy and self-care is both important and necessary rather than wrong. You may have the ingrained belief that service is the best way of expressing your love for others and demonstrating your own worth, and therefore you fear becoming unlovable if you refuse to do something or if you are not wholeheartedly devoted to someone else's needs.

On the flip side, however, you might also expect others to behave this way; if they don't, you then think that it's because they don't "truly" love you.

You Were Forced to Do Something You Didn't Want to Do, and Your Needs and Emotions Were Invalidated

If, when you were a child or a teenager, you were led to believe that your feelings, needs, or wants were irrelevant and that you had to leave them aside to please others, you may have internalized that belief and carried it with you into adulthood. For instance, if you didn't like hugging or kissing certain people when you were a child, and, instead of offering you other equally polite options, you were urged to kiss and hug them without anyone acknowledging your discomfort, you may have become an adult that agrees to certain things, even if you don't want to, just because you feel that what other people want is more important than what you want.

Emotional Blackmail Was Used to Invalidate Your Needs and Emotions

"I'll be upset if you cry." "If you don't do this, your dad won't want to spend any more time with you." "Don't be sad, or else your mom will be sad because of you." If you got these kinds of messages growing up, you may have learned that showing how you felt was wrong. You might have internalized the belief that expressing your emotions, saying that you don't like something or that you don't want to do something, or expressing your anger or sadness will bring negative consequences; you may even believe that those consequences are legitimate. This kind of conviction predisposes you to be easily mistreated and manipulated by an abusive person, because the table is already set for the manipulator: The victim believes they don't have the right to express how they feel and may even justify being emotionally or physically punished by the manipulator or emotional blackmailer.

You Were Taught That Saying No Was Wrong

If, as a child, you were assigned tasks without explanations and scolded if you expressed disagreement, you may have internalized two things: First is the belief that saying no is wrong because it has a negative effect on others. Second is the way you treat and speak to yourself, because as I mentioned earlier, children mimic how they are treated and spoken to for the rest of their lives. This is why it is so important that you scrutinize what hurtful messages you have internalized and relearn how to treat and speak to yourself in a healthy and fair way. If your feelings were invalidated when you were a child or you didn't feel heard, you're quite likely to reproduce that pattern, invalidate your own feelings, or fail to listen to what you really want.

That may be why you automatically say yes to other people's requests without stopping to ask yourself whether you really want to agree or not. You don't take time to listen to yourself and determine if you really want or are able to do what you've been asked to do.

Listen to what you're being asked for, stop for a few seconds, ask yourself if you want or are able to do it, and only then give an answer. This is a habit everyone should incorporate into their lives as soon as possible.

You Were Told That True Love Was Always Unconditional

Regardless of whether you learned it from what you saw at home or from rom-coms, this idealistic, unreal, and highly toxic idea of love has been quite harmful for everyone.

This conception of love is a double-edged sword: On the one hand, it may have led you to believe that, if you love somebody, you have to unconditionally devote yourself to them (regardless of the cost and even if it goes against your values and needs). On the other, it may have convinced you that, if that person doesn't love you unconditionally, it's because they don't love you at all.

This widespread belief can cause considerable pain when it comes to showing love to your partner, your family, and your friends.

Identifying this supposition, deconstructing it, and understanding that this is not love is essential. Love needs boundaries. In order to be real, safe, and long-lasting, love requires understanding and empathy toward yourself and others.

In this model where "what's mine is yours, what's yours is mine, and everything belongs to everyone or else it's not love," we make the serious mistake of obliterating everyone's individuality. Everyone's personal space, intimacy, potential for growth, and basic needs seem to disappear. The self is blurred. There is no difference between yourself and others. Therefore, you might become confused about your own identity because you're no longer aware of where you begin and where you end, or where the other person begins and ends. This could lead you to develop deeply dependent relationships where, if you lose the other person, you also lose yourself.

. . .

If you have experienced any of these situations or have been taught these beliefs, you probably feel guilty or selfish when you try to indulge yourself with some self-love and self-care. A good way of checking whether you're truly being selfish is by analyzing your upbringing. If you relate to any of the examples presented in this chapter, remember that the line between selfishness and self-love might seem distorted from your perspective. Judging yourself so harshly is not only wrong, but it's also unfair for you.

* **5** *

DECONSTRUCTING BELIEFS

When we are little, we are taught, first of all, to believe anything authorities tell us, be them priests, our parents. . . . Then, we are taught to reason our beliefs. Freedom of thought works the other way around: first comes reasoning and then our decision to believe in what our reasoning considers adequate.

— José Luis Sampedro

A Real-Life Case

Marga and Carlos, a married couple aged 45 and 48, came to my office seeking couples therapy because they had spent the last couple of years constantly arguing. Marga had suffered several uncontrollable fits of rage, reacted aggressively, got easily irritated, and had cut off all kinds of sexual contact with her husband. She was feeling very bad about herself because she believed that her husband and their two daughters were the most important part of her life, but she felt that, no matter how hard she tried, her family was falling apart because of her moodiness and attitude.

"I can't control my anger attacks and my bad mood. I get upset very easily, and anything can turn into an argument with Carlos. Then I reconsider and realize it was all silly, but it's too late because we have already argued, and I said some things I later regret. I feel terrible and I apologize, but the damage is done. Carlos and I are both strong-willed people, and we have always debated and defended our own ideas, but we have never disrespected or yelled at each other as we do now. When we had arguments when we were younger, I remember that we'd each explain our point of view, sometimes a bit heatedly, but later we'd reconcile and forget the whole thing. Besides, I've started lashing out at my girls when I'm moody. I'm very strict and I can't stand it if they don't do their chores right away, so I lose my temper quite quickly. I don't want to be a bad mother, but I don't know what else to do."

Marga began crying when she uttered the words "I don't want to be a bad mother." She was trying to look after her family by getting fully involved in things and by investing every second of her spare time on them. However, she felt deeply frustrated when she realized that fights and discussions were becoming more frequent and hurtful.

The Therapeutic Process

In the first sessions we analyzed their couple dynamics, their communication style, the roles they had established, and the beliefs behind those roles. Marga had several beliefs that made her feel guilty when she was supposed to set boundaries. She believed that if she didn't spend all her spare time on her daughters, she wouldn't be a good mother, and if she didn't please her husband, she would be a bad wife. She also feared losing their love or being rejected by them.

Once we identified those beliefs, we began working on deconstructing them and substituting them for beliefs that allowed her to build healthier relationships with her family and adopt a role where she felt more comfortable and happier. In the first part of the therapeutic process, we focused on helping her understand that caretakers need to look after themselves first before they can look after others; in other words, if she didn't indulge in some self-care, her situation would never improve.

At first, Marga felt so guilty; she couldn't conceive the idea of spending some time on herself rather than on her family, but she was able to gradually identify and acknowledge the beliefs that fostered her guilt, and later redefined what selfishness, self-love, and family love meant for her.

In the second phase of the process, Marga worked hard on strengthening her self-esteem with the help of an exercise called "The pillars of your life," a fully introspective process designed to underscore the specific personal needs she was neglecting. In order to carry out this exercise, she also had to learn that wants and needs are not the same thing.

Wants are those things we *desire* or would like to have, but we don't consider them essential, and they generally don't last for a long period of time (or are felt too intensely). Needs, on the contrary, feel more visceral, stand the test of time, and are perceived as something necessary to achieve fulfilment and self-actualization.

Marga began to understand that, in her attempt to please everyone, she was neglecting herself, which had emotional consequences that manifested as moodiness, irritability, anger, and sadness. She forced herself to give what she thought she should give to her family in order to be a good mother and wife, while neglecting her own needs and failing to ask herself if this made her happy.

Once she realized that the only way to be her best self with her family was by acting without neglecting herself or forcing herself to do things, even if that required spending less time on her family but making it better quality time, she started doing things for herself.

After working on her beliefs, we established behavioral guidelines: Carlos and Marga reorganized their schedule so that the house chores and the parenting responsibilities were evenly distributed and allowed both to have time for self-care. It didn't require significant changes; having just three more free hours a week helped Marga feel better about herself and feel more relaxed and more able to put family issues into perspective. She also became more patient with her daughters and noticed that anger no longer took ahold of her. Although she was spending less time with her daughters, when she was with them, she was in a better mood and her attitude and predisposition were more positive, which made her feel better about her role as a mother.

The therapeutic process helped Marga deconstruct certain beliefs that caused her constant discomfort and anxiety—such as the idea that "true love is unconditional," that "saying no makes you a bad mother and wife," or that "satisfying your needs is an act of selfishness"—and allowed her to exchange them for healthier ones. She understood that being generous can sometimes be selfish, and that being selfish can actually be an act of generosity in certain circumstances. She learned that agreeing to everything did not make her a better wife or mother, and that she would never feel satisfied and fulfilled if she prioritized looking after others before looking after herself. She made a commitment to take better care of herself so she could be better at taking care of others, and she has kept her word until this day.

Self-Actualization

One of the most useful exercises for self-awareness and personal growth is an activity called "the pillars of your life," (**albacardalda.com**) which helps us reflect on the most important parts of our lives by allowing us to analyze how we relate to them and to the people around us. It helps us identify the key parts of what we need to feel self-actualized and become the best version of ourselves: the kindest, happiest, most understanding, resilient, tenacious, persistent. . . . Each of us has certain traits that arise only when all our needs are being met, when we feel in tune with ourselves, and when we have found our balance.

Many people think that spending time on themselves is selfish, and that setting their needs aside to indulge and fulfill the needs of others makes them better human beings. However, they don't realize that only when they feel self-actualized can they become the best version of themselves, and that the people around them could benefit from that, because the direct consequence of feeling good about ourselves is that people enjoy being around us.

When we feel complete and satisfied, our attitude and mood improve. We become nicer, happier, more generous, proactive, optimistic, and confident. . . . We complain less, envy other people less, act less fussy, and become less suspicious, obsessive, and critical. Also, we should consider that our attitude can be highly contagious. Several psychological studies have shown that when we spend time with joyful, enthusiastic people, our mood improves, and we feel more joyful and enthusiastic ourselves. On the other hand, we have already discussed the emotional impact of the way in which we treat others. Therefore, when we feel self-actualized and our needs have been met, we are in a better mood and have a better attitude toward others, which has a positive effect on them (even if we were investing more time and effort on them earlier, when our attitude was more negative).

Just like Marga, sometimes the best we can do for others is to be a bit more selfish and spend some time on ourselves so we can feel self-actualized and act more positively toward other people. Engaging in excessive altruism, on the contrary, means that you might be doing it out of selfishness because you want to feel like a better, more useful, and more lovable person. But you might be doing it with a negative attitude because, in doing too many things for others, you are neglecting yourself.

If you want to start looking after yourself and work on your self-actualization without feeling selfish, you must remind yourself over and over, like a mantra, that looking after yourself also implies looking after others. This helps shed a more positive light on prioritizing your own needs, which will not only improve your life, but the lives of those around you.

* 6 *

WHAT SHOULD WE DO ABOUT GUILT?

In the end, we are our choices.

— JEFF BEZOS

Using Guilt as a Manipulation Device

Earlier in the book we discussed the cultural beliefs we grew up with that make us feel guilty when we try express our boundaries and say no, as if we didn't have a right to do it or as if we were violating some sort of ethical code by respecting ourselves.

Guilt and fear are two of the most common control and manipulation mechanisms there are. They have been used since the beginning of time by the media, religious institutions, cults, and governments to manipulate people for their own benefit. The level of ignorance of a group of people is what makes it possible to subjugate them: Ignorant people are easier to manipulate through fear than educated people. Ignorant citizens lack critical thought, and without the ability to think critically, there is no freedom of thought; if there is no freedom of thought, there is no freedom at all. Ignorant people are, therefore, subjugated people.

The same happens in our interpersonal relationships: It's easy to use emotionally ignorant people. Individuals with underdeveloped emotional intelligence can be effortlessly subjugated through fear and guilt because they're unable to question their truth.

If you want to avoid being manipulated, you must work on your emotional intelligence so you can identify when someone is trying to use those mechanisms against you.

Let's discuss guilt, then. There are two types of guilt:

Healthy or Adaptive Guilt

- This is the type of guilt one feels after making a mistake or violating ethical codes or norms.
- It's proportional to the consequences of the damage or mistake.
- It drives us to repair the damage and prevent similar behaviors in the future. It also allows us to learn from our mistakes and take responsibility for the consequences of our actions; in other words, it helps us grow as individuals.

Unhealthy or Maladaptive Guilt

- It's the kind of guilt we feel even if we haven't made a mistake, caused some damage, or violated any ethical codes or norms.
- It's disproportionate to the harm or mistake (it's usually too harsh and is accompanied by rumination).

- It's destructive rather than constructive, since it negatively affects our self-esteem and self-image.

If you carefully analyze the guilt you're feeling, you'll improve your emotional intelligence, which will not only protect you from being manipulated, but also force you to question the beliefs that could lead you to codependency and toxic relationships. To do so, you can start by making three basic questions that help clear your mind on whether you're judging yourself fairly or excessively.

The diagram that follows is a basic but quite useful tool to help you look closely at many of the dynamics of your personal relationships and determine whether or not they're based on the kind of guilt that forces you to agree to things you don't want to do, accept things that hurt you, and allow others to transgress your boundaries and violate your rights.

The answers you get will inevitably lead you to additional reflections: Do I often feel guilty about certain things even if I shouldn't? Do I constantly feel the need to apologize over things that aren't actually hurtful? Am I consciously letting someone manipulate me? They will also make you ask yourself: Am I making someone feel guilty when they shouldn't? Has someone's behavior really violated my rights, or does it only bother me to give up my privileges? Am I upset because of what they did, or does it bother me to get no for an answer? The answers to these questions will also raise further questions, and that's how we gradually weave a net made of the yarn of self-knowledge, which forges our emotional intelligence and supports our ability to handle our own emotions and understand the emotions of others, as well as our ability for leadership, resilience, self-control, empathy, tolerance of frustration, and critical thinking that allows us to evaluate our behavior and the behavior of others. These make it easier to set boundaries and decide which of the other people's boundaries we accept, which helps us build healthy, fair, and respectful quality relationships.

Reason Versus Heart

In the words of Blaise Pascal, "The heart has its reasons, which reason does not know." It often happens that, although we understand why we feel the way we feel, and even though we know we "shouldn't" feel this way, our feelings persist.

In the case of guilt, we're able to identify the misconceptions that hold these feelings and acknowledge why we shouldn't feel guilty; however, getting rid of guilt seems impossible. Being familiar with the theory doesn't necessarily make us better practitioners, and this is what makes therapeutic work so difficult: It's not only about reasoning, but also about feeling. It's the eternal struggle between the heart and the reason: We know we must love and value ourselves, but that's not enough to make us feel like we are really loving and valuing ourselves. We know we shouldn't let other people's opinions influence us, but that's not enough to prevent us from feeling upset when someone criticizes us. We know we shouldn't feel guilty about setting boundaries, but we still feel it when we do.

To understand why this happens, let's consider the role played by the brain structures in charge of these functions. The neural circuit in charge of reasoning and decision-making (the prefrontal cortex) is almost structurally and functionally independent from the neural circuit in charge of emotions (the limbic system). Each circuit works independently, as if they had nothing to do with each other and that this didn't imply terrible contradictions and headaches for us. Additionally, the negligible connection between both systems is not balanced: There are a lot more connections from the limbic system to the prefrontal cortex than the other way around. In other words, when it's time to make decisions, our emotions have a deep influence in our reasoning, whereas our reasoning has little influence in how we feel.

This is why in cognitive-behavioral therapy (CBT), in which we try to change how we feel by influencing our thoughts, we need to repeat the therapeutic strategies over and over to strengthen the neural pathways that go from the prefrontal cortex to the limbic system so we can compensate for how they work in the opposite direction.

Hopefully, one day neuroscientists will find a way to create equal connections between these two circuits—even if it's with duct tape—that can save us from those horrible internal conflicts (and, with a little luck, also save us some money on therapy).

Frustration, Our Old Friend

One of the skills that emotional intelligence helps us develop is the ability to tolerate frustration. Tolerance of frustration is a basic necessity if we want to change or learn anything, because when doing so, one thing is for sure: We'll make one mistake after another, and things will go wrong hundreds of times, so we'll have to endure feeling frustrated on hundreds of occasions as well. That's why it's necessary to accept frustration from the very beginning as our partner in any change or learning process. It's going to be there from the start and until we reach our goal, so we'd better accept it from the get-go. This will help us tolerate it more easily and get up every time we fall so that we can keep going.

You learn to write by writing and to walk by walking, so it's only logical that you can learn to set limits only by setting them. There is no other way. Therefore, once you've learned how to question your guilt, you should start practicing, even if at first you still feel guilty. Expecting not to feel guilty just because you know you shouldn't feel guilty will only lead to frustration and to abandoning your goals after only a few attempts.

As I said before, heart and reason do not go hand in hand, so trying to align them will require many "failed" attempts before we can finally make it. You might feel that those attempts are useless because they are unsuccessful, but you couldn't be more wrong. In fact, they are crucial for achieving real change. They are part of the experiences we need to have so that our brain can tolerate that amount of guilt and become somewhat desensitized to it. You should focus only on the fact that, after a few attempts, that guilt will blur until it (almost) disappears.

The same thing happens when you try to take on a new habit, such as a sport. If you've never been specially interested in practicing sports, at first it can be quite difficult because you might feel lazy, you feel sore, results are not immediate, your technique feels inadequate. . . . If you think that, once you start exercising, you'll feel motivated, it will feel effortless, you'll look like a professional athlete, and you'll see results in no time, those unrealistic expectations will be quickly unfulfilled, and you'll feel inclined to give up. However, if you accept from the start that the process will take time and effort, that you might not do things as good as you'd like because of your lack of experience, that you will not get the desired results immediately, and that on many days you'll feel lazy and won't feel like leaving the couch to work out, then you'll be more likely to achieve your goal.

Both in the process of setting and respecting boundaries, and of redefining and changing our limiting beliefs for liberating ones, we'll need to keep the same principle in mind: Only by repeatedly doing and thinking about things in a different way will it stop feeling weird or forced, and finally feel normal and become automatic.

7

THE DOSE MAKES THE POISON

The trick to balance is to not make sacrificing important things become the norm.

– Simon Sinek

"Boundarism"

Paracelsus was a controversial doctor, astrologist, and alchemist from the 16th century whose contribution to medicine was the creation of the first drugs and medications made with chemicals and minerals. After many years of experimenting, he came to the conclusion that every substance can be either a remedy or poison, depending on the dose.

When it comes to setting boundaries, the dose also makes the poison: We must find the balance between being totally uncompromising and being entirely submissive.

Another way of turning a remedy into poison is by adding to it the suffix *-ism*. When we add this suffix to certain words that initially represented positive concepts that could have provided a remedy, it's as if we upped the dose so much that we turned it into poison. From liberal comes liberalism, from fan comes fanaticism, from capital comes capitalism, from service comes servilism, and so on and so forth.

Boundarism is the term I use to express a radical position when it comes to setting boundaries. It's a misunderstanding of the concept of boundaries, the uncompromising "all or nothing" position, the dose that turns the remedy into poison.

Respecting our rights, saying no, and attending to our needs is not in direct conflict with courtesy, kindness, and camaraderie. We may often want to be accommodating with the people we love, we practice kindness (something that definitely improves our relationships with others and makes us feel good about ourselves), we want to do things out of camaraderie, and we choose to yield in certain circumstances to enjoy healthy interactions with others. That's another way of caring for others and showing our love for them, but it's healthy only if we are aware that this is where it's coming from: a place of wanting to care for others without neglecting ourselves. This is absolutely necessary if we want to have quality relationships, which is why it's essential to find the sweet spot, the right dose. This is no easy task, and finding it depends on our emotional intelligence, our ability to listen to ourselves and others, our willingness to accept how we feel and how others feel without judgment, and our ability to be flexible enough to distinguish what is important from what is not.

A specific tool that can help us identify this sweet spot is setting thresholds. Let me give you a simple example of how this works: Imagine someone asks you for a favor. A co-worker asks you to cover for them next Friday evening. You're torn between being a good colleague and your need to rest after working the whole week; in other words, between meeting the needs of others or your own. If you don't know what to do, you can set thresholds; this implies asking yourself questions and rating from 0 to 10 the answers to how much you wish to do something, how much you'd enjoy doing it, or how much it would hurt you to do it. You must also set a threshold (6 or 7 is usually a good idea) that helps you decide whether to agree or not. For instance, in this case, you could ask yourself the following questions: "From 0 to 10, how much effort would it take me to cover for my co-worker on Friday evening? How tired am I?" Once you've given an honest answer, if you got less than 6, you might consider saying yes. If it requires more effort on your behalf, you could consider saying no.

Using the same example, another way of setting thresholds would require asking yourself, "How much will it affect me to do this? Nothing, a bit, considerably, or a lot? Will I need to sacrifice something? Does it interfere with my own goals?" If you answer "considerably" or "a lot," you should consider saying no. If your answer is "nothing" or "a bit," you could consider saying yes.

These questions help us learn to listen to ourselves right when someone asks us for something, instead of just replying automatically. After this initial consideration, you should also take into account at least three more factors that may influence your decision.

Who's Asking?

Is this person usually nice to you or not? What's your relationship with this person? Is there some sort of workplace hierarchy in play? How has this person responded when you have asked them for help?

How Often Do They Ask You for Favors?

Do they ask you for a favor only every now and then, or have they started asking frequently? It's important to keep in mind that, if you've done three favors in a row for someone, the neural pathways formed in the prefrontal cortex of that person make them start believing that they're entitled to ask for favors and that it's your obligation to agree to them; that is, certain roles are being established. To avoid this, try not to do three favors in a row (or at least not without letting the other person know that this cannot become a habit).

Why Are They Asking?

Is it something important or irrelevant? Have they asked you because they are unable to do it or because they don't want to do it? Following the previous example, you could ask yourself: Has my co-worker asked me to cover for them because they're going out with friends or because they have to take their child to the doctor?

Considering these three aspects will help you give answers tailored to each situation and find a balance based on the context.

• • •

When someone starts going to therapy, initially they find this extremely difficult, because doing this analysis every time someone asks for a favor or invites us to do something can feel somewhat forced at first. It might not come naturally to you because that's not the way you usually do things (and that's also why you need to change your approach). However, if you repeat this exercise several times, thanks to the brain's plasticity, you'll be able to create new neural connections that will eventually turn it into an automatic habit.

If you want to understand how this process works in your brain, try remembering when you learned how to drive.

You probably remember the first time you got in the driver's seat and tried going for a ride. Paying attention to so many things at the same time—pressing the clutch pedal while you shift into gear and releasing it slowly while you press the gas pedal, turning on the turn signals, looking in the rearview mirror before changing lanes, and driving forward slowly while turning the steering wheel—was quite overwhelming. At first, paying attention to everything at the same time required a great effort, but after a while—and after the car stalled a few times—you start doing it without thinking. Why? Because repeating each step slowly and very consciously allowed your brain to create and strengthen new neural connections until they were so strong that driving became automatic. Now you just get in the car, start the engine, and drive away without giving it much thought.

This happens in your brain every time you repeat over and over something that is new to you; it can be anything, like a dance move, a new drawing technique, new words in another language, or a new habit. You generate new neural connections that strengthen with each trial and error, and once you have repeated the same process enough times, those new neural pathways become so strong that the thing that was difficult at first has become automatic. This is what we call "learning."

The same thing happens when we learn new ways of thinking or acting: At first, we have to reflect on it a lot, so it takes a lot of time; after repeating it a few times, we learn to do it almost without even considering it.

Folk Psychology

The healthier our self-esteem, the less dependent we are on the approval of others. As we validate and value our own opinions, we become less vulnerable to what other people think of us. However, it's impossible to deny our gregarious nature, our biological need of belonging to a group.

Ever since *Homo sapiens* began walking the Earth—about 2.5 million years ago—belonging to a group allowed human beings to establish relationships based on trust and solidarity through cooperation networks that also guaranteed their survival. If, on the contrary, the group refused to accept an individual, an early death awaited the latter for sure.

Even though society has changed a lot since then, the human brain has remained the same for the last 50,000 years. Although we no longer need to fight dangerous predators or take turns stoking the fire, we have the same social mechanisms for survival that our ancestors had—namely, needing external approval from the group to become part of it. Although the need for approval is innate, we must observe how each of us experience it and find a middle ground that allows us to feel accepted by the group without failing ourselves or being dishonest with ourselves.

Some phrases taken from the folk psychology movement (a school of thought that is excessively positive and unrealistic and is especially popular in social media) convey the message that we can totally control the effect that other people's words and actions have on us. However, this goes against our social nature and the biological needs derived from it (that is, our need for approval from the group, whose function has always been to keep us alive).

Instead of making us believe that we can fight our own nature and forcing ourselves to stoically endure an unlimited number of unpleasant behaviors and words from others, which lead to great pain and frustration, there are three things we can do that are a lot more effective when it comes to dealing with our need for approval:

1. *Acknowledging our needs.* We can only work on the things we accept, which is why acknowledging that we need to feel approved by others helps us do something about it and even regulate how much we need it.

2. *Learning to distinguish the things we can control from the things that we can't.* Accepting that some things are out of our control (for instance, other people's feelings or opinions) allows us to focus our energy on taking action only on the things that do depend on us (such as acting according to our principles and respecting those of others) and to let go of responsibilities that do not belong to us.

3. *Deciding who is part of our group.* We don't need every single person's approval—if you feel like you do, you should work on regulating it. We only need the approval of the people we consider an important part of our lives. If we observe the people whose approval we seek, it will lead us to consider whether it should necessarily be them or if we should devote our time and energy to other relationships that could be more gratifying.

These three actions will force you to actively make decisions that address your affective and emotional needs. Then, instead of sticking to the premises of folk psychology, you can stick to premises that remind you that you are entitled to set boundaries and to decide to end hurtful relationships.

This is the biggest act of self-love you can do for yourself. It doesn't mean that messages such as "no one can make me feel bad if I don't allow it" cannot be useful in certain situations, but it's important not to generalize them or try to apply them in all contexts. For instance, this message can be helpful if an unknown driver in another car opens their window and insults you, but not if your co-worker speaks to you with contempt and disdain every single day.

In the first case, you don't have a relationship with the other driver, so you understand that their comments are not personal and are probably a result of their own frustration and mood rather than of how they feel about you. Also, it's an isolated incident with a person you'll probably never see again. In this case, the message from folk psychology might be useful: You won't let it ruin your day, you'll ignore it, and you'll carry on with your life as usual.

However, in the second case, you do have a (work) relationship with your abuser and have to interact with them every day, which implies that you'll be abused often. In a circumstance such as this one, it's not as easy to stop their daily behavior toward you from having an impact on your mood and even your self-esteem.

In such cases, it's quite common to end up feeling sad, upset, moody, humiliated, and even anxious if you are unable to end the abuse. This is not a sign of weakness! On the contrary, if you experience these emotions, it means you're a human being with a healthy brain, since they are the result of existing connections between the prefrontal cortex (the reasoning) and the limbic system (the emotions). If you didn't have an emotional reaction to these situations, it would mean that those two parts of your brain are disconnected (and that you're a psychopath).

This is why it's important to accept that the unpleasant emotions we feel when someone treats us badly are normal, healthy, and even useful, because they drive us to set boundaries. This is when we must exercise our right to decide whether we'll allow being abused or whether we'll set boundaries to stop it.

. . .

When we try to apply these kinds of messages from folk psychology in all circumstances, we run a significant risk: We might end up blaming ourselves for the emotional effect of being mistreated by others and feeling even worse than how our abuser makes us feel because we're unable to stop feeling bad. It's a double whammy! On the one hand, it's unfair to blame the victim for feeling painful emotions after being abused; on the other, it's unfair to exempt the abuser from all liability.

Acknowledging our vulnerability as human beings is essential. We don't have to go through life as if we were ruthless soldiers on the warpath: tough, insensitive, and invincible. That's not who we are. We are vulnerable, emotional people, and we need both to look after others and to be looked after.

The words and actions we use to treat others and the ones they use to treat us should always be respectful, but that's the responsibility of the person who speaks or acts, not of the recipient. If someone disrespects us, hurts us, or oversteps our boundaries, this will naturally have an emotional effect on us, and it would be unfair to make us believe that it happened because we were not strong enough to prevent it and that the person who abused or mistreated us bears little or no responsibility.

One of my clients, a 32-year-old woman called Sandra, is the perfect example of someone who blindly believed in folk psychology.

Sandra told me that, ever since she was little, her relationship with her older sister, Patricia, had been difficult. When they were little, Patricia would insult Sandra, and Sandra would cry. But their parents merely said, "Don't be silly! If you're going to react like that every time your sister says something nasty to you, you're in for it!" Later, in her early teens, Sandra was bullied at school. Her teacher told her parents that it might be good to take her to the school's therapist. During those sessions, the therapist taught her that "things will only affect you if you let them."

The psychological intervention was not focused on strengthening Sandra's self-esteem. She wasn't taught to set boundaries or told that it was her classmates who were wrong. Nor did the therapist explain that Sandra had the right to be respected and to say, "No more." Also, the teacher didn't approach the people bullying her to show them the effects their behavior could have on Sandra's mental and emotional health, she didn't try to teach them about empathy and respect, nor did she remind them that they shouldn't treat others the way they wouldn't want to be treated.

None of that happened. Sandra was the only one who was held responsible for how she felt, so she grew up believing that: "If things affect me, it's because I let them affect me. It's no one's responsibility but mine." This mantra led her to allow all kind of abuses from her sister, her colleagues at work, her friends, and her partners, while she held on and tried to "develop a thick skin." She thought she didn't have the right to set boundaries or to distance herself from people who disrespected her. Instead, she believed she had to accept those behaviors and deal with them herself, regardless of how abusive or hurtful they were. She was constantly turning the other cheek.

After some time in therapy, Sandra finally understood that she was entitled to and capable of making decisions, and that it was up to her to decide whether to hold on to relationships with people who hurt her and took advantage of her or not. She understood that it wasn't necessary to be the "patriotic warrior" who stands on the front lines of relationships that hurt her, that saying "no more" was her prerogative, and that it didn't make her weak, merely a person with self-love.

Cognitive Biases

A cognitive bias is an erroneous way of interpreting the information surrounding us that influences our behavior, our way of thinking, and the way in which we make decisions.

There are several kinds of cognitive biases. One of the most common ones is thinking in absolutes: Things are either black or white, good or bad. This failed way of thinking hugely limits our reasoning and our problem-solving abilities.

Cognitive biases also influence folk psychology, which is why we find it so hard to accept that not everything depends on us or on others.

There are several things you can do to avoid depending excessively on others and to stop their words and actions from hurting you as badly: You can learn to modulate the intensity with which they affect you, to heal emotional wounds that make you react disproportionately, to work on your complexes, to balance your sensibility, to find alternative ways of interpreting what happens around you, etc. But you also need to learn to set boundaries without feeling guilty and to be selective about the people you forge relationships with.

When you do everything in your power to make a relationship healthy, but still feel dissatisfied with what you get in return, it's time to make a decision that prevents you from postponing suffering; in other words, either both parties redefine their needs and negotiate, or you make the decision of distancing yourself from that person or even choose to end the relationship. It's essential to know exactly where your responsibility in the relationship beings and ends, and where the other person's responsibility begins and ends.

* 8 *

WHERE TO SET THE BOUNDARY

Freedom is [. . .] a movement of consciousness that leads us, at certain moments, to utter one of two monosyllables: Yes or No.

— Octavio Paz

Negotiable and Nonnegotiable Boundaries

After discussing what boundaries are and what they aren't, quality relationships, limiting beliefs, and how our relationships influence our life and our perception of happiness, we have yet to discuss the most important part: identifying our boundaries and learning to communicate them.

It's quite common that our way of operating is incompatible with another person's way of operating, but that doesn't mean that either of us are bad people. There isn't always a culprit, a toxic person, a narcissist, or a psychopath involved. Somctimes, people simply don't work well together, and we need to recognize it so we can make the best decision for both parties. Also, each person has their own needs and rules of the game. There are no good or bad, right or wrong ones; they are simply each person's own.

Boundaries—whether our own or someone else's—shouldn't be judged; they should be respected and that's that. If they are compatible with ours, we can have a relationship with that person; if, on the contrary, they are incompatible, we have the right to choose to have a relationship with that person or not. This of course, goes both ways; that is, if the other person disagrees with our rules of the game, we should accept and respect their right to distance from us.

If you want to identify what your rules and boundaries are, there are two powerful tools you may find very useful: emotions and self-awareness. Your emotions will act as a compass that will let you know whether you find something pleasant or unpleasant, whereas self-awareness will let you determine the deeper sense and meaning of those emotions, which may help you name and understand your boundaries.

Everyone experiences six basic emotions: happiness, sadness, fear, disgust, anger, and surprise. Only one is pleasant, four are unpleasant, and the last one, surprise, can be both. This means our brains are much more prepared to identify dangerous things so we can stay away from them than to reveal things that may be pleasant. If we ignore unpleasant emotions (as folk psychology suggests we do), we stop listening to the danger signs, which is like being lost with a broken compass. Thus, we should open space for and tend to all our emotions.

Once you have identified your boundaries, it's important to distinguish the two main types: those that you would never let anyone transgress under any circumstance—the nonnegotiable boundaries—and those you can be flexible about, depending on the circumstances—the negotiable boundaries.

Nonnegotiable Boundaries

Nonnegotiable boundaries are essential to make us feel physically and emotionally safe and for relationships to work. They are linked to our needs, values, principles, and dignity.

Although everyone has their own nonnegotiable boundaries, some of them should be universal: no form of violence, whether it's physical or verbal; respect; no infringement of our freedom or rights; and honesty, to name a few. These are some of the boundaries that you must never compromise on or negotiate under any circumstances. If they are transgressed, the consequences must be swift and severe.

Identifying your nonnegotiable boundaries and not yielding is absolutely essential to setting effective boundaries. Knowing what is fundamentally important to you will allow you to be more flexible and tolerant with what is not so important, thus moving away from the extreme of "boundarism."

Negotiable Boundaries

Negotiable boundaries are those that you can be more flexible about, because, although they are based on your preferences and desires, they don't threaten your physical or emotional integrity, they don't compromise your dignity, and they aren't rooted in your values or principles. Therefore, they give us a certain margin to adapt as well to other people's needs and tastes and keep a good balance in our relationships.

When the negotiable boundaries of two people are incompatible, they can negotiate them and come to an agreement that is satisfactory for both.

Three Steps for Acknowledging Your Boundaries

1. *Take time to think about your negotiable and nonnegotiable boundaries.* Keep in mind that being inflexible in certain areas allows you to be flexible in other areas, to adapt to other people's circumstances, to come to an agreement with other people about the codes that support your relationships with them, and to maintain your relationships despite any existing differences.

2. *Identify the relationships where your boundaries are not respected or where you find it harder to say no.* It's helpful to analyze each of your closest relationships to identify the ones where setting and respecting boundaries is more challenging. There are some people who make it hard for us to defend our rights, whether it is because they are aggressive or manipulative, or because they command so much respect that they make us forget our own self-respect. This usually happens when we run into a pattern that reminds us of someone who was very demanding of us.

For instance, if you had an authoritarian father, it's possible that other figures that remind you of him (older, strong-willed, and confident men) make you feel small and make it harder for you to communicate your boundaries assertively and to say no to their requests.

The same is true in reverse: You might respect some people's boundaries more than others'. Take a moment to reflect on this and question whether you respect other people's rights of your own free will and moral stance, regardless of whether they ask for it or not. This is one of the most challenging self-awareness exercises, because it requires a great capacity for self-observation, and, above all, humility, honesty, and emotional intelligence.

3. *Identify specific situations where you find it harder to set boundaries and say no.* Just like communicating your boundaries and saying no might be harder for you with some people than with others, certain contexts also play a part in this. For instance, it's usually harder to say no when you're surrounded by a group of people who have already said yes (i.e., when you feel peer pressure) or to give a negative opinion in front of several people instead of doing it in front of just one. Being able to identify the circumstances in which we find it harder to

set boundaries helps us pay better attention to them and find concrete solutions to problems.

"Min-Plus"

When we communicate our boundaries to others, we're in fact setting limits to ourselves and telling ourselves: "This is what I'll tolerate, and this is what I won't." This first boundary has only got to do with us, and we must act accordingly to look after, protect, and respect ourselves. This means that we may sometimes have to make painful decisions that are essential for our mental health and well-being, such as distancing from someone or ending a relationship.

Imagine you open a food-delivery business. At first, you decide to be available 18 hours a day to boost your company. After a year, you've built a substantial customer base, a stable income, and a reputation for serving quality food, but you're completely burnt out. You make the decision of working fewer hours (because the current work rhythm is unsustainable, and you haven't been able to spend quality time with your family), so you let your customers know that, from now on, you'll only offer your services for 12 hours a day, instead of 18.

This is when you'd realize that there are two kinds of customers: those that sympathize and understand, and those who don't and become upset. Most of the people from the first group will keep on recommending your food and appreciating your services, while a few might stop buying from you if your new schedule is incompatible with theirs, but continue recommending your food and appreciating your services.

Despite their initial discomfort, some of the people in the second group will finally accept that you're a human with needs, just like them, and will continue buying your food, while some of them will be so upset they will no longer buy from you. The latter are the undesirables, the kind of customers any service provider has had to deal with, who make you want to cry your heart out; it's the kind of demanding and contemptuous customers, those that—for some strange reason—believe you're not worthy of their respect and act as if you'd been born to serve them. Trust me when I tell you that you shouldn't be interested in attracting them, and losing them is no real loss, but an actual win. This is what I call a "min-plus," minuses that are actually pluses.

The same thing happens in personal relationships: Sometimes, a loss is really a win. Although it may sound contradictory and is painful at first, we need to learn to let go of people who are unable to respect our boundaries or sympathize with us. We must accept that it's impossible to be in everyone's good graces, because protecting, looking after, and being honest with ourselves is not compatible with getting along with people who mistreat us. If you want to prioritize your mental health, before pleasing and making those people happy, you need to have a healthy self-esteem. If you fail to accept this, you'll stay surrounded by abusers.

It's normal to experience certain min-pluses when you start setting boundaries, but doing so is only a filter to cleanse your social environment. It may be hurtful at first, but you'll heal. However, it's quite likely that most of the people who obtained benefits from your lack of boundaries will need some time to adapt and understand what is happening. They may feel upset, confused, or disoriented at first by this new relationship dynamic, and may even angrily berate you for having changed instead of remaining the same.

In fact, that's the idea.

After giving them time to adapt and reflect, the people who love you in a healthy way—regardless of whether they understand your limits or not—will either accept them and respect them, or they may try to negotiate them with you.

Therefore, you should take for granted that right after setting limits, it's quite common to be confronted with accusations and long faces, but it's necessary to go through that stage and remain steadfast in your goal long enough for others to adapt. This is definitely the hardest stage of the process, but once it's over, everything else falls into place.

* 9 *

ASSERTIVENESS AND COMMUNICATION STYLES

We are what we do to change who we are.

— Eduardo Galeano

What Is Assertiveness?

In general terms, assertiveness is defined as the ability to express emotions, opinions, and thoughts in a way that is respectful to one's own emotions and to the emotions of others. In other words, it's a way of communicating quite honestly without being aggressive, while being kind enough without being submissive.

This definition applies only to the communicative dimension of assertiveness. It could be said that it's the first level of assertiveness, but there is a second level: *being* an assertive person, which encompasses plenty of other abilities and constructs beyond the expressive dimension. Being assertive is an attitude, a way of connecting to others and to oneself, of behaving and feeling and experiencing what happens around us. It's a lifestyle in which honesty, respect, and a sense of justice influence not only our expressions, but also our actions and feelings.

Thus, it's important to distinguish between having assertive behaviors and being an assertive person. While the former is related only to the communicative level, the latter includes not only the behavioral dimension, but also the cognitive and emotional ones.

How Can You Become Assertive?

"Being" a certain way is always much more complicated than "behaving" a certain way. However, behaviors can lead the way to becoming who we want to be.

One of the factors that influences the most our way of being is how we communicate. Language, which represents one of the main aspects of communications, has a decisive influence on how we think, feel, and relate to others, and even on how we interpret and shape our reality. That's why it's so relevant to every aspect of our personal and social life.

Language is a powerful tool that forges, destroys, and builds realities: If something is not named, it doesn't exist, whereas anything that has a name becomes real. This explains why, for the social justice initiatives fighting to change things that are deeply ingrained in our culture and our society (such as misogyny), one of the key and most powerful elements for promoting changes in people's mentality is reshaping language with the purpose of raising awareness among the general public of all the misogynistic attitudes, beliefs, actions, laws, institutions, traditions, and expressions that we had normalized (many of which are still normalized).

Changing the individual use of language of many people changes the collective imaginary, which in turn changes the societal perception of reality. That's how ideas, beliefs, cultures, and societies are changed.

Similarly, modifying our language is a very powerful and efficient strategy when we're working on any psychological skill or aspect. Changing how we express activates a psychological domino effect that causes a chain reaction of increasingly deep and complex changes, such as the dynamics in our relationships, our self-concept, our thoughts, and even our emotions.

Communication Styles

When you engage in a therapeutic process with the purpose of modifying a certain part of your behavior, the first step is to be familiar with your starting point—that is, with your current actions, thoughts, and feelings (the three elements that support our behavior)—or your point A.

Once you know exactly where you are, you need to know exactly where you're going, which is your goal, or point B.

To go from point A to point B, you need to establish an action plan made of smaller and concrete objectives (or sub-targets) with specific deadlines that progressively drive you closer to your final goal.

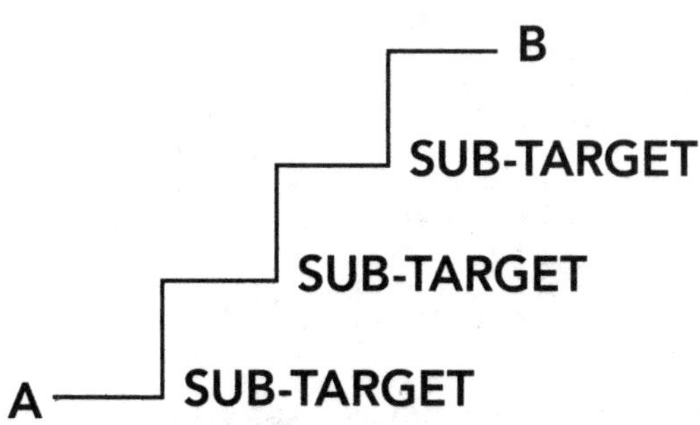

Your point B is being able to set boundaries in your relationships in a way that is both healthy and assertive.

Point A will be different for everyone, which means that you will need to begin by identifying your starting point or communication style.

One of the easiest ways of identifying and classifying different communication styles is the two-axis model, where the horizontal axis represents how much you defend and respect your own rights, and the vertical axis indicates how much you defend and respect the rights of others. This model will not only help you identify your own communication style, but also the communication styles of the people around you.

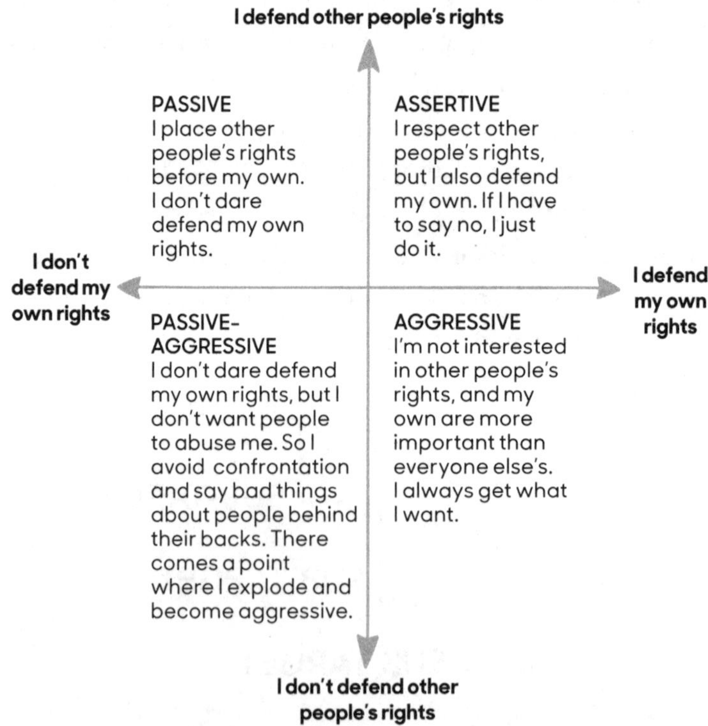

Based on this model, there are four basic communication styles:

Passive Style

This person doesn't defend their own rights and instead prioritizes and defends the rights of others. They don't openly express their emotions and feelings out of fear, thus invalidating themselves because they feel that their thoughts and emotions aren't important, or they fear being criticized or judged. Therefore, tensions, frustration, and resentment build up and cause feelings of anxiety, sadness, guilt, and anger.

They usually use words or phrases such as: "Don't worry," "It's fine," "It doesn't matter," "Maybe," "Sorry" (very often used), "I don't mean to bother you."

Nonverbal language: Their communication style is characterized by looking down or avoiding eye contact, a low voice volume, occupying little space, not gesturing with their hands and arms, and a closed posture.

Aggressive Style

They only defend their own rights and have no respect for the rights of others. They are hostile in their expression and disregard other people's feelings. They generally feel anger and hate.

They often use words or phrases such as: "You should . . ." "You don't know much about . . ." "You'd be better off if . . ." "You've got to be kidding me."

Nonverbal language: They steadily keep eye contact, with a stern expression; they speak loudly; they tend to speak quickly; they take up a lot of space (e.g., they sit with their legs spread apart or invade other people's personal space); their gestures are threatening, like when they point at someone with their index finger while speaking, or they bang on the table; their posture is rigid and tense.

Passive-Aggressive Style

They don't defend their own rights but try to enforce them through manipulative mechanisms that prevent other people from imposing their own. By not allowing themselves to express their emotions, their anger, frustration, and sense of injustice accumulate and translate into a hypocritical and dishonest form of manipulation (guilt, punishment, or plans of revenge).

They tend to use words or phrases such as: "Well, that's up to you," "I won't bother you anymore," "No, I'm all right, don't worry," "Do whatever you want."

Nonverbal language: Their communication style is usually a combination of the passive and the aggressive, depending on the moment and the people involved.

Assertive Style

They defend and uphold their rights as much as the rights of others. When they communicate, they keep in mind the emotions and assertive rights of others as much as their own, and they express their opinions honestly without imposing them or invalidating the opinions of others. They understand that their own freedom ends where someone else's freedom begins, and vice versa. They don't mistake assertiveness with having the right to mindlessly say whatever comes to their mind, nor do they mistake freedom of speech with having the right to give their unsolicited opinion on anything or anyone. They know very well where the line between one thing and the other is; in other words, they act respectfully.

They usually say words or phrases such as: "I believe that . . ." "I'd like it if . . ." "I want to . . ." "Let's do this . . ." "How can we figure this out?" "What do you think?"

Nonverbal language: Their communication style includes looking at people in the eye with a calm and relaxed expression, and for no more than 7 to 10 seconds at a time; using a perfectly audible volume without raising their voice; gesticulating with their hands and arms, without invading the other people's personal space; communicating fluidly; keeping an open posture: shoulders slightly back, back straight, chin up, and arms relaxed when they're listening.

Once you have identified your starting point and your final goal, you can start drafting the action plan so you can successfully get from one point to the other.

However, before you go any further, you should take into consideration one of the basic tenets of psychology: Everyone has different circumstances and qualities, and we all function differently. Therefore, there is no single way of going from point A to point B: Every person will project their own way depending on their own starting point and individual qualities. (In general terms, self-help books don't take this into consideration and try to impose a unique model that doesn't really work for everyone.) Someone with an aggressive communication style will need a different path than someone with a passive style. Someone who struggles with change will need more time than someone with a high degree of adaptability. Someone who is continually punished and manipulated by their peers will need to work harder on their beliefs and feelings of guilt than someone who feels supported by their family during this process, and so on. Each person's conditions and qualities are as diverse as there are people on the planet, which is why a one-size-fits-all recipe is impossible to find.

The Fundamentals of Assertiveness

Assertive behaviors are mainly based on the 10 basic assertive rights I mentioned earlier and on only one obligation. Remember that you have:

- the right to express feelings, emotions, thoughts, and needs

- the right to be treated with respect and dignity
- the right to disagree
- the right to say no
- the right to want something
- the right to not want something
- the right to change your mind
- the right to make mistakes
- the right to decide upon your own life, body, and time
- the right to establish your own priorities

And your only obligation is:

- respecting that others have these same rights

However, as I mentioned earlier, assertiveness isn't just about having the ability to communicate in a certain way. It also requires having a set of skills, beliefs, behaviors, and ways of thinking and feeling. In order to become assertive, it's essential to have previously worked on certain aspects of our personality that form the basis of assertiveness.

This idea can be better understood using an iceberg model, which is laid out in the image that follows. Underneath authentic assertiveness lie all the elements that represent the base of the iceberg: values, respect for assertive rights, beliefs, moral principles, communication skills, emotional

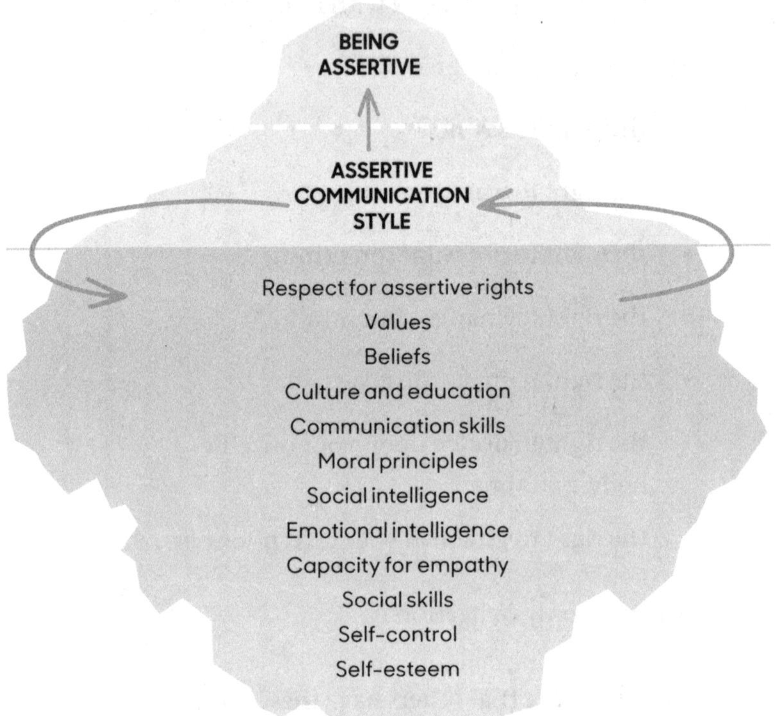

intelligence, social intelligence, culture, and education, social skills, capacity for empathy, self-awareness, self-leadership skills, and, of course, self-esteem. These factors influence our ability to behave assertively. Therefore, self-awareness is key to achieving this and any other personal goals we set for ourselves. Once we are familiar with all of these aspects of ourselves, we may be able to identify any potential biases or shortcomings that hinder assertiveness. A good exercise is trying to question each of these aspects in ourselves.

I have previously discussed the limiting beliefs that make us feel guilty when we prioritize our needs or desires. Only by identifying this type of beliefs can we work on them and make them nonlimiting. Therefore, it is essential to spend some time analyzing the beliefs we have about ourselves, others, and the world at large; identify those that we might need to deconstruct; and then reconstruct healthier beliefs in their place if we want to design a road that takes us from A to B.

The same thing happens with our moral values and principles: If we want to be assertive, it's essential to be respectful, fair, and kind. Thus, reflecting upon our values and principles, and behaving with integrity, is also necessary to become assertive.

Additionally, keeping in mind how our culture and our education influenced us helps us understand our communication style better and, consequently, makes it easier for us to modify it.

Our degree of emotional and social intelligence, and our communicative and social abilities are also determining factors. The set of skills underlying these constructs forms the basis of cognition and the ability to relate assertively. Therefore, understanding ourselves in these areas will also reveal important information about whether we need to train in any of them.

Self-leadership is the ability to direct our thoughts and actions. This allows us to say no when we want to say no and to say yes when we want to say yes; to act in accordance with our values; to honestly express what we think and feel; to set boundaries when we need to, etc. Observing whether we are capable of self-leadership will also reveal whether we need to work harder on some of these aspects in order to reach the necessary level to be assertive.

Finally, at the base of the iceberg, we find our self-esteem: the foundation of all our behaviors, thoughts, and emotions. Self-esteem is formed by our self-concept, self-evaluation, self-acceptance, and self-respect, and it shapes our entire life. Working on the aspects that may be weakening it and limiting us is essential to becoming truly assertive, since an assertive person necessarily has a healthy self-esteem.

On the top of the iceberg, we find two levels: having an assertive communication style and being assertive. These are not the same thing: We can have an assertive communication style and not be assertive ourselves, although the reverse is not possible.

We become assertive people when assertive communication transcends other levels and we act, think, and feel assertively.

A person who communicates assertively but is not assertive knows very well what they "should" say but feels unpleasant emotions when doing so. For instance, they know they have the right to say no, but if they do, they consider themselves selfish. However, assertive people know and feel that they have the right to say no, and when they do, they remain calm and don't feel guilty or selfish.

Someone with an assertive communication style knows that they must respect when someone cannot or does not want to do them a favor and will probably respond assertively but feel upset about it. However, a really assertive person emotionally and cognitively respects it when someone cannot or does not want to do them a favor and accepts it without a problem, without judging or feeling offended by anyone.

Assertive people respect assertive rights, not only from a rational point of view, but also from an emotional one: They feel that they are acting in a healthy, honest, empathetic, and fair way; they don't see themselves as guilty, bad, or selfish people for doing so; and they acknowledge that others have these same rights.

. . .

In summary, if you want to reach the tip of the iceberg of assertiveness—in other words, if you want to *become* an assertive person—you must necessarily work on the aspects that form its base. Doing so will allow us to have an assertive communication style (first level of assertiveness), which will cause a domino effect of changes in the way we relate to others, which in turn will influence the way we relate to ourselves and all the deeper aspects that form the base of the iceberg. This feedback between the base of the iceberg and the first level of assertiveness, sustained over a long period of time, leads us to reach the top of the iceberg: becoming comprehensively assertive people.

* 10 *

COGNITIVE-BEHAVIORAL STRATEGIES TO COMMUNICATE YOUR BOUNDARIES EFFECTIVELY

[I]nstead of teaching [her] to be likeable, teach her to be honest. And kind. And brave. Encourage her to speak her mind, to say what she really thinks, to speak truthfully [. . . .] Tell her that if anything ever makes her uncomfortable, to speak up, to say it, to shout.

— Chimamanda Ngozi Adichie

Now that we are familiar with assertiveness, albeit theoretically, it's time to get down to business.

As in any psychological process, the most effective way to achieve improvement is to act on both the cognitive and behavioral levels. The cognitive level encompasses our mental processes and thoughts, while the behavioral aspect involves our actions. The cognitive-behavioral approach promotes changes in the way we think and interpret reality while implementing changes in our behaviors. Thus, we achieve profound and sustained changes over time.

In this chapter, we'll focus on those cognitive-behavioral strategies that can improve our assertiveness skills.

It's normal to find it very difficult at first to carry out the tactics explained below. It's important to respect the time for training, the trial-and-error period when results usually consist of more errors than successes, but which is necessary to improve and reach your goal. You will also encounter emotions that are difficult to manage, such as fear, guilt, insecurity, or rejection from people who will dislike that you start setting boundaries.

The Three Golden Rules of Effective Communication

When it comes to setting boundaries and saying no, we must take into consideration three basic rules:

Say It Clearly and Firmly, Without Beating Around the Bush

There is a Spanish proverb that says "If you have to say no, do it right away." It's true: When someone crosses a line or you just want to say no to something, it's best to do it as soon as possible, without beating around the bush. It's like pulling off a bandage: It will definitely hurt, but the slower you do it, the more intense the pain will be. It's best to do it gently, but with one quick motion, and that's it.

The best way to set boundaries and say no is to do it with love, but clearly and firmly, without giving too many explanations.

When you beat around the bush or try to justify yourself too much, you make two basic mistakes: First, you're suggesting between the lines that the fact that you don't feel like doing something or that certain behaviors bother or hurt you is not reason enough to say no or to set boundaries; thus, you invalidate yourself. Second, for every explanation you offer the other person, you give them a chance to find a solution and continue insisting; in other words, the more explanations you give, the more they will insist.

Example:

"Shall we go for a drink?"

"Um . . . well . . . the thing is, I don't have any money."

"Oh, don't worry. It's on me! You'll pay next time!"

"Well, I appreciate it, but it's already a bit late."

"Relax! It'll be just one drink and then we'll leave. It'll be nothing. Come on!"

"But I told my wife we'd have dinner together, and she's waiting for me."

"Well, I'll pay for your taxi once we've had our drink, and you'll definitely be home in time for dinner."

"Yeah . . . well . . . okay . . ."

If instead of justifying yourself or making excuses you just firmly and clearly say no, the other person won't be able to offer solutions or insist.

Example:

"Shall we go for a drink?"

"I don't feel like it today, but thanks. Maybe some other time!"

Set Proportional and Consistent Consequences

A boundary is not a boundary if there are no consequences when someone crosses it. The consequences must be in line with the damage caused or the seriousness of what happened; in other words, they must be proportional. For instance, you cannot treat someone who is late for an appointment—even if it's the second or third time—in the same way as you would treat someone who has physically or verbally assaulted you. Crossing that last boundary is much more serious than crossing the former, so the consequences should also be more severe.

The other condition of this kind of consequences is that they must be consistent. If you have previously told someone the effect that crossing a boundary would have, you should always follow through, without exceptions. Otherwise, you will lose all credibility and send the message that "you can do anything you want to me." Therefore, if you choose to make the consequences explicit, you should be able to follow through.

Third Time's the Charm

When it comes to accepting favors or giving in in certain situations, you must keep in mind this rule: After the third consecutive time that something happens in a certain way, people start taking for granted that this is how things should be. Therefore, the moment you stop doing it, they perceive it as unfair. This doesn't happen when you refuse to do things from the very beginning.

For instance, when John got a new job, one of his co-workers asked him if he could help him upload some data into a company program. John agreed to help him with that task because, although he already had enough work catching up with the new job, he didn't want to look bad in front of his co-workers. The following week, the same person asked him for the same favor again, and John agreed for the same reason. On the third week, the same co-worker asked him again, and John said yes one more time. John was getting tired of having to do someone else's work, so he decided next time he would refuse. But, to his surprise, his co-worker only said: "I'll leave the data that needs uploading on your desk, John. Thanks! See you on Monday!"

John's co-worker assumed that John would do the task because it had already become a habit. And this upset John greatly because it made it even harder for him to refuse to do someone else's work, even if it wasn't his responsibility. However, he plucked up his courage and, the following week, when his co-worker gave him the data that had to be uploaded to the program, John told him that, unfortunately, he could no longer take on this task because it was taking time away from his own work. His co-worker merely replied politely, "Oh, it's fine, don't worry," but he's never spoken to John again, except for greeting him and saying good-bye to him cordially.

Although there is no doubt that John's co-worker was cheeky and that John's intentions were good, he made the mistake of agreeing to do someone else's work for them on more than three occasions, without even mentioning that it took quite a bit of his time or clarifying that he would agree to do it only once, and avoid committing to it any further. When John told his co-worker he could no longer upload the data into the program, the other party perceived it as if he were refusing to do something he had already committed to do.

Undoubtedly, it was John's co-worker who misinterpreted the situation, but without getting into who was right or wrong, this kind of situation occurs in daily life, and you can do something to avoid ending up in John's shoes. You can refuse to do the favor before the third consecutive time you're asked, or, if you choose to agree, make it clear that you won't always be able to do so.

The "As If" Strategy

As I've said before, when we practice assertive communication, we inspire positive changes in deeper aspects of ourselves and thus generate positive feedback. Walking the path of change in this direction—from our behavior to our deeper self—is much easier than doing it the other way around—from our deeper self to our behavior. That's why mental health professionals use this resource very often to modify complex aspects of their clients' personalities or behaviors.

This strategy consists of acting as if you're already an assertive person in order to actually become an assertive person, which happens thanks to the feedback mechanism discussed before. However, I would like to point out that this approach doesn't work for every single aspect of our personality or behavior that we want to change. Every reader should use their common sense to identify whether it's useful or not, but it's certainly a technique that helps improve many psychological aspects.

Starting to act as if you're already an assertive—or friendly, attractive, confident, eloquent—person will bring you closer to becoming one. However, in order to succeed, you need to implement a specific strategy: the "as if" strategy.

This method consists of dividing the assertive behavior (or any other skill you want to work on) into levels and climbing the ladder gradually until you reach your goal.

You can begin by dividing the assertive behavior into seven basic social skills:

1. the ability to say no
2. the ability to take no for an answer
3. the ability to ask for favors and make requests
4. the ability to refuse favors and requests
5. the ability to express both positive and negative feelings and opinions
6. the ability to respect other people's positive and negative feelings and opinions
7. the ability to initiate, maintain, and end conversations

After that, different levels are determined based on the skills acquired: not assertive at all, slightly assertive, moderately assertive, and completely assertive.

- *Completely assertive*: All skills have been acquired and are implemented frequently.
- *Moderately assertive*: There are difficulties acquiring one or two skills, or they are implemented on some occasions but not on others.

- *Slightly assertive*: There are difficulties acquiring between three and five skills, or they are rarely implemented.
- *Not assertive at all*: There are difficulties acquiring more than five skills or they are almost never implemented.

Based on these definitions, you can identify your current level and carry out the strategy as follows:

1. Assess where you are right now (for instance: *slightly assertive*).
2. Recognize the skills that you find it difficult to acquire or implement (for instance: saying no, taking no for an answer, asking for favors and requests, refusing favors and requests, and expressing both positive and negative feelings and opinions).
3. Choose one (or two) of these skills and set daily goals that you should ideally try to achieve over a period of two weeks. For instance:
   - Over the next two weeks, every single day respond with a no to requests.
   - Over the next two weeks, every time you get a no for an answer, take time to interpret it, keeping in mind everyone's assertive rights, in order to develop a

more respectful and understanding internal discourse around that no.

— I recommend you keep a calendar or goal chart at hand where you can write down every time you achieve each goal and how you feel or what you think about it.

4. After spending a couple of weeks working on these goals, choose another two and repeat the process (without neglecting the ones you have already worked on). Carry on like this until you have covered all the skills. As you work on each objective, it's important to write down how you feel, the changes you perceive, and the reasonings that emerge as your behavior changes. This will serve as a guide that helps you identify which factors may need more work or attention.
5. Once you have worked on all the skills, reassess yourself to determine which ones you have fully embraced and which ones you haven't fully acquired. The ones that you find most difficult are probably those that involve emotions you also find difficult to manage, so it's important to ask yourself which beliefs are sustaining them.
6. To maintain those behaviors, keep a record of your thoughts, your emotions, and any difficulties that arise, as well as of the conflicts

they might generate, among other things. This will help you gradually move from the behavioral to the cognitive and emotional levels by working on all the necessary aspects to begin communicating assertively and then becoming assertive yourself.

The "Mental Map" Strategy

There are two concepts that are very useful when it comes to setting boundaries assertively and—above all—effectively: mental maps and empathy.

Let's recall the concept of the mental map: Everyone has their own model of the world, which includes filters through which we interpret reality. A mental map is each person's unique, subjective way of understanding the world, others, and themselves. It is developed based on our education, genetics, culture, experiences, beliefs, values, ambitions, expectations, personality traits, and emotions. Understanding this means accepting that each person interprets reality in their own way and, based on that, builds their own truth, which is not the only truth, just "their" truth.

Thus, even if we disagree with someone who stands up for a truth that doesn't match ours, keeping in mind this premise and trying to act consistently with the assertive rights can be quite helpful (especially when we're dealing with people whom we care for). Similarly, we must demand that others treat us and our truth with the same respect.

When we assume that each of us has a unique and subjective mental map, we can avoid the mistake that almost everyone makes: treating others as we would like to be treated, instead of treating them as *they* would like to be treated. This brings forward the concept of empathy. Empathy is often defined as the ability to put ourselves in the shoes of others and treat them as we would like to be treated. However, this definition of empathy is flawed because it implies putting ourselves in someone else's shoes while maintaining our own mental map, rather than adopting that person's mental map. In the end, this is not very useful. In order to put ourselves in someone else's shoes, it's essential that we see the world from the perspective of their own mental map. This will allow us to develop true empathy. Understanding this will give us an enormous advantage when we interact with people in general. Knowing the map of the people we interact with makes communication easier; helps us understand their reasoning and behaviors without judging them; predisposes us to listen to and understand them, rather than become defensive; and allows us to reach a consensus with them more easily.

Similarly, if you want to set boundaries in your relationship with someone, you'll find it very helpful to keep this in mind, because it will help you make them understand the need for boundaries by using terms from their own mental map. This strategy is one of the most effective communication strategies because people only change if they feel an urgent need to; that is, if they have an internal motivation to do it.

Otherwise, changes will be artificial or unsustainable. With this strategy, you can strengthen their motivation to make real and permanent behavioral changes.

However, I wouldn't recommend making the immense effort of being empathetic with everyone you want to set boundaries with, because, generally speaking, it's their responsibility to respect your boundaries without needing further explanations that help them understand those boundaries. And, if they don't want to respect them, they can simply walk away—or give you the chance to make the decision of walking away yourself. However, when it comes to relationships with people from whom you can't easily distance yourself—such as your parents, children, in-laws, co-workers, among others—explaining the rationale behind your boundaries in terms of their mental map (especially when it comes to children and teenagers) is a very clever and efficient strategy.

Analyzing Someone Else's Intentions

When you become familiar with someone else's mental map, you can understand why they act the way they do. Based on that, you can set boundaries in one way or another.

It's important to take into consideration the other person's intention when they did something that upset you. Just like you wouldn't react similarly when someone steps on your foot accidentally versus when someone else does it deliberately, you won't react in the same way to a boundary being transgressed "accidentally" or "unintentionally" rather than "deliberately."

When someone says or does something that upsets you, considering their mental map can help you find different explanations to their behavior and identify their intentions.

Once, a Colombian friend of mine came to visit me in Barcelona. After spending a few days in the city, I took him to see the north of the peninsula. In Donostia, I took him out for drinks, and there we met some very nice Basque guys. My friend told a story about how he had been mugged by some criminals and how he got away by using his wits. One of the Basque guys told him, "Woah! You son of a bitch! Ha! Ha! Ha!" laughing in surprise at the sagacity my friend had shown in the situation he described. My Colombian friend turned to me, his face contorted in anger and disbelief. "Did he just call me a son of a bitch?" I quickly explained to him the meaning of that expression in that context; the Basque man's intention was to praise his reaction to the mugger, and his words meant to represent his admiration. My friend had interpreted the expression from the point of view of his own mental map—as a vulgar and blatant insult—rather than from the point of view of the Basque man's mental map.

This confusion almost led to a heated argument, and misunderstandings in communication are the source of many conflicts. That's why understanding the mental map of the person you're talking to can save you a lot of problems and help you understand the intentions behind their words or actions. This will help you, on the one hand, to avoid taking their actions or words personally, but rather as a result of their way of seeing and interpreting the world, and, on the other, to modulate your reactions depending on whether their intentions were good or not.

* 11 *

EFFECTIVE COMMUNICATION STRATEGIES FOR ESTABLISHING AND NEGOTIATING BOUNDARIES

Diplomacy works in negotiations; diplomacy is getting others to do what we want them to do, and to do it gratefully.

— Dale Carnegie

More Than Just Assertiveness

As you train yourself in cognitive-behavioral techniques, you will find it easier to express yourself assertively. However, if you want your boundaries to be truly effective, assertiveness won't be enough. You must also learn certain effective communication strategies, which imply a linguistic and gestural programming that communicates trust, firmness, and respect. Without them, setting boundaries can be more detrimental than beneficial to your relationships. Let's focus on a specific example.

Sonia and Paula work together on the same sales team at the company and need to communicate frequently throughout the day. Sonia is very warm and affectionate, and, when she talks to someone, she tends to get quite close, even to the point of physical contact. Sometimes, since she's very spontaneous, she interrupts the other person without realizing it to express her opinions. Paula, who is more introverted and thoughtful, prefers to keep her distance, doesn't like it when people touch her while she speaks, and hates it when they won't let her finish speaking when she's expressing her ideas.

The way Sonia communicates with Paula has made Paula increasingly annoyed, and she has started experiencing anxiety when she goes to work.

One day, Paula decides she can't take it anymore. She read in a psychology blog that setting boundaries is necessary and a very positive thing to do, so she has decided to tell Sonia that she finds her invasive way of communicating with her uncomfortable, that she finds it exasperating when Sonia touches her arm, and that she thinks it's very rude to interrupt her when she's speaking.

It's true that Paula would be assertively setting a boundary without disrespecting or judging Sonia, and that she would be expressing her complaint as a personal opinion rather than as a judgment. However, the effect of conveying her message in this way would probably create tensions between them and would make it harder for them to continue working smoothly and with a positive attitude. In other words, in doing so, Paula would set her boundaries assertively, but not effectively.

. . .

When we don't know how to communicate our emotions or thoughts both assertively and effectively, we might only come up with ways of doing so that are unkind or even rude. This leads us either to remain silent and repress our emotions because we don't want to sound rude, or to communicate them thoughtlessly. When we suppress our emotions and avoid expressing them, far from reducing their intensity, we intensify them and excessively activate our limbic system.

When this happens, the overload starts looking for ways to escape, and we either explode like a pressure cooker, experience a fit of anger or anxiety, or somatize the whole thing. On the other hand, if we communicate them thoughtlessly rather than assertively, we can cause harm and damage our relationships.

Clearly, neither option is preferrable. Formulas for assertiveness, effective communication strategies, and nonverbal communication cues help us express our boundaries in a way that can be received both kindly and respectfully, leading to a greater rate of acceptance. Kindness and respect, together with a firm and calm nonverbal communication style, are key in the persuasiveness of these techniques, so we must never forget them if we want to use these techniques effectively.

In the next chapters I'll introduce some of the most effective strategies that communication experts, linguists, and psychologists have developed.

Nonverbal Communication

Nonverbal communication accounts for between 65 and 80 percent of the information we convey. We express a lot more with our gestures and facial expressions than with our words. Everything we do or avoid doing communicates something about us: our mood, our emotions, our personality, our attitude, our motivations, our preferences, if we approve or reject something . . . and even our self-esteem. We may stop communicating verbally, but we can never stop expressing ourselves nonverbally through our gaze, body posture, use of hands, facial expressions, speed of movement. . . . Apart from expressing countless things about ourselves, what we communicate nonverbally can also influence other people's behaviors, attitudes, and moods.

Let me tell you a story. Once, I arrived quite exhausted at my destination after a very long and eventful trip. My phone—in which my bus ticket was saved—was stolen, so I had to buy a much more expensive bus ticket than the one I already had, I left much later than I had planned, and to top it all off, the road was closed for hours because a landslide had caused an accident.

When I finally arrived at my destination, I was in a terrible mood, so I went into the first hostel I found open so late at night. The only thing I wanted was to lie down in bed until the next day. I went inside with a bored look on my face, and skipping all formalities, I blurted out coldly and rudely, "Hi, I need a room." In contrast, the person who welcomed me that night at the hostel reception was one of the kindest people I have ever met. Jorge, as he was called, far from responding with the same attitude with which I addressed him, replied to me in the best possible way, with a warm smile, a friendly tone of voice, and overflowing kindness from every pore. In the few minutes it took him to process my reservation, he completely changed my mood. It just took five minutes for his positive attitude to rub off on me and make me feel much better (and, of course, treat him and everyone else there kindlier). The next day, when I realized there had been a mistake with the payment of my reservation, I was much more forgiving than I would have been in any other circumstance.

It's a fact that people who convey kindness and confidence—which can only be achieved through nonverbal communication—inspire others to adopt a similar attitude toward them.

• • •

Although nonverbal communication strategies that convey kindness, confidence, and friendliness can be very helpful most of the time, unfortunately they will not always be the ultimate solution. There will be times in which we'll need to convey other kinds of nonverbal messages, such as respectability, firmness, and authority.

Part of communicating our boundaries effectively is being able to distinguish when and how we should express ourselves in one way or another. When there are inconsistencies between what we say and what we express nonverbally, what prevails is what we convey in the latter. Therefore, when communicating our boundaries, it doesn't matter how clear our verbal message is if we don't back it up with nonverbal communication strategies that convey confidence, firmness, credibility, and a certain authority. Otherwise, it won't resonate with our audience.

If your words say, "I will not tolerate you disrespecting me," but you're hunched, your voice is shaky, the volume of your voice is almost imperceptible, and you avoid looking the other person in the eye, you can be sure that they won't take you seriously, because what you're actually communicating is, "If you keep on disrespecting me, there will be no consequences, because I'm afraid of what you'll think of me and because I don't believe I deserve respect." When the verbal message doesn't match the nonverbal message, people believe the latter. Therefore, in order to demand respect, you need to be able to convey respectability. If you want to inspire confidence, you must know how to convey confidence. And, if you want to be given credit, you need to know how to convey authority.

The following strategies will elaborate on how to combine your words with appropriate nonverbal language that reinforces what you're communicating verbally.

Active Listening

A good communicator is, above all, a good listener. If you want to negotiate boundaries and reach agreements that help you communicate with your audience, you must first learn to listen so that you're able to:

- understand the other person's motives
- become familiar with their mental map
- build arguments based on the information and values of the other person's mental map to make them more understandable for them
- encourage emotional and cognitive openness in others so that they can understand your motives

If you feel like the person you are talking to is listening with the intention of understanding you (without counterattacking, for instance), your emotional system and the brain structures that regulate your social behavior keep you calm, confident, and mentally open, which is necessary for reaching agreements and solutions in any conflict. If, on the contrary, you feel like the other person is not paying attention to you and only wants to present their arguments without even trying to understand yours, you might become defensive or even aggressive. At this point, the conversation will no longer be aimed at finding a consensus, but rather each party will try to defend their position tooth and nail, and the goal of both will be to prove they're right, rather than to find a solution. This will completely block the process of negotiating boundaries and seeking consensus.

Active listening promotes what neuropsychologists call "cognitive flexibility," one of the most complex brain abilities that allows us to view a situation from a different perspective than usual and quickly adapt to the changes required by the environment. In other words, it enables us to adapt without much effort to the demands of life and survival—nothing less than the adaptive capacity that Charles Darwin described in his theory of evolution, but applied to the field of psychology.

However, this ability is not only useful for negotiating boundaries, but also, the greater a person's cognitive flexibility, the greater their ability to think creatively and unconventionally in any circumstance, which makes it easier for them to solve problems quickly and effectively in every aspect of their life.

Mentally flexible people are those who find solutions to unexpected events that come their way without becoming bitter or letting their mood be affected by the little everyday problems that may arise. Thus, if you want to be that kind of person, one of the best ways to start working on it is by actively listening to others without attacking them, especially when their point of view is totally opposite to your own.

Walkie-Talkie Strategy

Active listening is so simple that it's hard to understand why people find it so difficult to do, since it consists only of keeping quiet and listening.

A strategy that can make it even easier to put active listening into practice is communicating like we'd do with a walkie-talkie. This tactic also eliminates the main factor that causes communication failures: interruptions.

This is how you implement the walkie-talkie strategy:

While the other person speaks, you listen quietly and try to understand what they are saying. You cannot speak until the other person has finished speaking; otherwise, the communication would be interrupted, and you wouldn't be able to hear the information in its entirety, just like when you're using a walkie-talkie.

When the other person finishes, you should make a brief pause before replying to make sure that they have really finished speaking and, in turn, show them that you are considering their message carefully, rather than rushing into a quick counterattack.

Then it's your turn to speak and the other person's turn to listen actively. That's it!

Paraphrasing

When the other person has finished speaking, you can ask a question that paraphrases their main idea to make sure that you've understood it correctly. For instance: "So, if I understood correctly . . . *[explain the idea in your own words].* Is that right?" This way, you confirm that you have understood the message correctly and also show that you've been listening attentively, which fosters a calmer and more peaceful attitude in the other person.

The Lie Detector

One of the biggest advantages of active listening is that it helps you develop the ability to identify incongruous verbal and nonverbal cues; in other words, you become an expert lie detector. If you suspect that someone is not telling you the whole truth, remain silent for three seconds while maintaining eye contact with them, and that will cause their reaction to give them away. If they lied, they'll start to give more explanations, change their story, or appear restless.

Nonverbal Communication in Active Listening

- *Keep eye contact.* Nothing shows disinterest more than looking away when someone's talking to you. Therefore, look the speaker in the face, not only to give them your full attention, but to show them that you're giving them your full attention.

- *Stand up straight and face them.* Keeping your back straight and your body facing the person speaking to you conveys that you're paying attention to what they're saying.

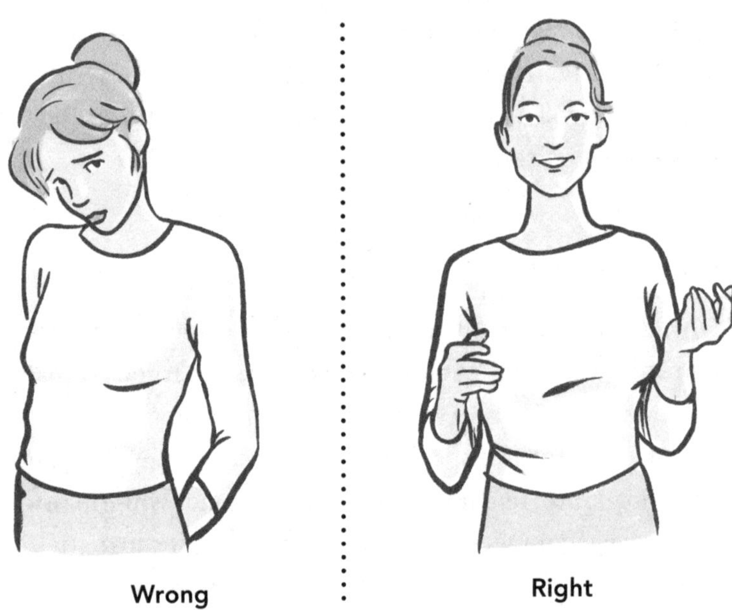

- *Keep your feet and legs pointing toward the speaker.* This indicates you're interested in the conversation. Conversely, pointing your feet to the side—especially if it's toward an exit—indicates discomfort or a desire to leave.

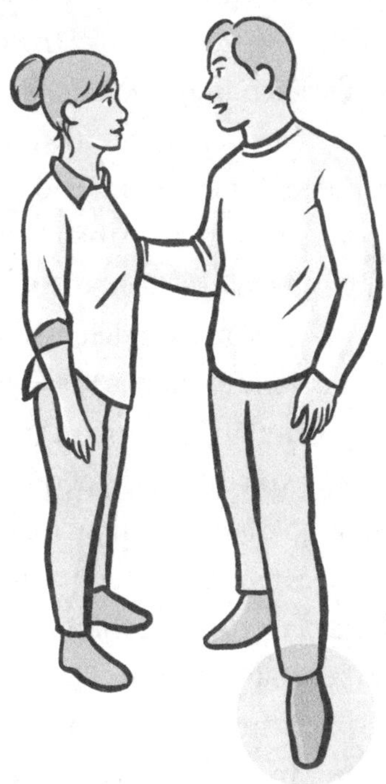

"I" Messages

I feel . . .
+ *when you . . .*
+ *You could . . .*

The most common mistake we make when we want to express our anger toward someone else is to blame them for our anger, and the immediate consequence of this is that the other person becomes defensive. When this happens, communication is bound to fail, because instead of having both parties rowing in the same direction to find solutions, each will row in their own direction to prove themselves right.

To avoid this common mistake, you simply have to replace "*you* messages" with "*I* messages," then propose a solution. This is a very practical tool when it comes to setting boundaries or asking someone else to change their behavior, because you encourage them to feel the need to make that change themselves, rather than the need to defend themselves. This is the only way for someone to change their behavior permanently. Demands, threats, and blackmail are not effective.

"*You* messages" focus on the person performing the action and hold them responsible for the feelings we're experiencing. These kinds of messages tend to express judgment, criticism, or disapproval of the person, rather than solely of the action itself. This, in turn, generates feelings of guilt, humiliation, or underestimation, which threaten the other person's self-concept and self-esteem. In response, it's inevitable that the recipient becomes defensive, tries to justify themselves, counterattacks, and resists changing their behavior. And this effect is multiplied when the message contains generalizations or categorical terms such as "always" or "never." The more "*you* messages" we use, the more likely it is that we end up in an argument with no chance of succeeding.

On the other hand, "*I* messages" focus on ourselves and are based on honestly expressing what we think or how we feel about a behavior, without any underlying judgments. They refer to the action and not to the person carrying it out. When we refer only to the facts, and not to the person who did the action, the recipient doesn't interpret the message as some sort of judgment, disapproval, or criticism, so they don't feel the need to counterattack, justify themselves, or resist changing their behavior to preserve their self-concept and self-esteem.

"*I* messages" are formulated as follows: "I feel that . . ." "I believe . . ." "This is how I feel . . ." "I think that . . ." When we use this formula, we speak from a position of absolute subjectivity, without condemning or judging the other person, or without imposing our point of view as an absolute truth. Yet we openly and sincerely express how we feel about the facts. That's why these kinds of messages can be very influential and persuasive, making it easier for the recipient to understand us better, agree to reach a consensus, and be motivated to change their behavior.

The third element in the equation of "*I* messages" is suggesting a solution or expressing what we would like to happen next.

Some examples of this kind of message:

- "I feel sad when you don't remember the important things I share with you. I would like you to pay more attention when I share things that concern me."
- "I don't think you've taken my feelings into consideration. Could you think about how this might make me feel the next time you're in a similar situation?"

- "I feel like you treat me with arrogance when you talk to me this way, and it hurts me. Could you talk to me in a less condescending tone?"
- "I feel ignored when you reply to messages on your phone while I'm talking to you. Could you put it away while we're having a conversation?"
- "I don't feel respected when you behave like that toward me. I would appreciate it if you didn't do that again."

	YOU Messages	I Messages
PURPOSE	They focus on the other person (the *you*).	They focus on ourselves (the *I*).
ACTION	They hold the other person responsible for our feelings.	They talk about the effect that the other person's actions have on us.
WHAT THEY COMMUNICATE	Judgment Criticism Disapproval of the other person Punishment Imposition	Honest and sincere feelings in response to a situation or action
WHAT THEY GENERATE	*Feelings of:* Guilt Humiliation Underestimation Threat to self-esteem and self-concept Need to defend oneself by counterattacking, justifying oneself, or resisting change	*Need for:* Self-evaluation Self-questioning Self-analysis Helping others Openness to change Less resistance Cooperation

	YOU Messages		I Messages
OUTCOME EXAMPLES	You never listen to me.	▶	I feel sad when you don't remember the important things I've told you.
	You're inconsiderate.	▶	I don't think you've taken my feelings into consideration.
	You're arrogant.	▶	I feel like you treat me with contempt when you talk to me that way, and it hurts me.
	You disappoint me.	▶	I feel disappointed when you act that way.
	You're rude; stop answering messages while I'm talking to you.	▶	I feel ignored when you reply to messages on your phone while I'm talking to you.
	You're very disrespectful.	▶	I don't feel respected when you behave like that toward me.

Whenever we use "*I* messages" and then express our need, what we convey is not perceived as a demand but as a request for help to feel better. And here's the key: When people receive a request for help rather than an imposition, their willingness to change their behavior is considerably greater.

Basic Assertive Nonverbal Communication Strategies

The most assertive nonverbal communication strategies (and the ones you'll need to use more often) are:

- *Keep your head up.* It's very important not to tilt your head, which is exactly what we do when we adopt a playful or flirtatious attitude because it makes us seem sweeter and more likeable. When you're trying to set boundaries, you must avoid those kinds of gestures, as they affect your credibility and authority.

- *Keep eye contact.* Avoid looking away but also don't keep eye contact for more than six or seven seconds at a time, so that it isn't perceived as an aggressive stare.

- *Use a medium volume and a firm but calm tone of voice.* Try to express your emotions honestly, without being aggressive or shy. If you want to add some authority to your verbal message, use a slightly lower tone of voice than usual, as lower tones convey more confidence and authority than higher tones.

- *Keep an open posture.* An open posture is one where the vulnerable parts of the body (i.e., those that are vital for our survival, such as the chest, neck, and abdomen) remain exposed. This kind of posture expresses confidence in yourself and in the other person. It's as if you were saying, "I trust you enough to believe that you won't attack me, but I also have enough confidence in myself to know that I can react quickly if you attack me and defend myself."

With this posture, you communicate a doubly positive message and neutralize negative verbal messages without contradicting them.

To have an open posture, keep your feet slightly apart, your head up, your back straight, and your shoulders slightly back. Avoid wearing scarves, and even unbutton the top button of your shirt, because that will help you convey your message.

- *Move your hands naturally and organically.* Occasionally show your palms, since this will help emphasize what you're saying and convey confidence and credibility.

We'll refer to this set of nonverbal cues as "basic assertive nonverbal communication strategies," which you can use to accompany most of the verbal strategies explained below, as it involves assertive, nonviolent, and effective communication. Therefore, unless a specific nonverbal communication strategy is mentioned, it should be assumed that using this set of nonverbal cues is the most advisable approach. However, if you need to reinforce your message depending on the context, or you don't want to convey a positive message with your body, I'll show you which elements you need to change according to what you want and need to convey at any given moment.

Using the Passive Voice

When we use the passive voice to express a message, we omit the person performing the action. Thus, by not explicitly holding anyone accountable, our message is not perceived as a personal attack or a direct order. For instance, instead of saying, "You have to finish this report by six," you could say, "This report must be finished by six." The latter will be interpreted in a much kinder way than the former.

"What's in it for me?"

Once you have mastered the mental-mapping technique from Chapter 10 and deduced what motivates and interests another person, you can shape the conversation to set your boundaries by showing the other person how they will benefit.

This strategy requires great emotional intelligence and empathy, but it's one of the most eloquent and effective techniques out there when it comes to effective communication. For instance, imagine your mother shows up unexpectedly at your house on a Sunday afternoon and opens the door with the spare key you gave her for emergencies. It upsets you that she did this because you consider it an invasion of your privacy and a lack of respect. You could literally tell her, "It bothers me when you come without a warning because I feel like you're invading my privacy, and I consider it disrespectful when you don't let me know beforehand." It would certainly be assertive, but it would probably be more effective to tell her, "Mom, if you're coming to my house, I'd like it if you'd let me know a little ahead of time so I don't make other plans with friends and I can spend time with you. Also, you wouldn't want to arrive and surprise me with my partner, right? I'm sure you'd rather not witness *that*. So, please, just let me know the next time you plan to come over." In short, whenever possible, it can be extremely persuasive to let the other person know the advantages of the boundary you are setting.

Offer Validation

"I understand your [the other person's right or need] . . ."
+ *"but I [your right or need] . . ."*
+ *"You could/we could [solution] . . ."*

There is a chance that, despite using "*I* messages," the other person will remain firm in their position and justify their behavior without any intention of changing it. As long as they're not overstepping any of your rights, they assume that what they're doing is totally legitimate and respectable, since it's equally valid for them to manifest their opinions and needs and act accordingly.

However, if this happens, you shouldn't give up but rather continue negotiating. You can use this technique to continue the conversation in a friendly and constructive tone, with the aim of narrowing the gap between your perspective and the other person's perspective, and trying to reach a consensus. This technique is based on showing you understand and respect the other person's rights and needs as well as your own, and suggesting a solution that both parties can agree on. The result is that the other person feels validated and respected, and will be more willing to question their motives and validate yours, reconsider whether both are carrying the same weight, and open up the possibility of softening their position.

Let's go back to the example of the phone:

- *[I message + proposed solution]:* "I feel ignored when you answer messages on your phone while I'm talking to you. Could you put it aside while we're having this conversation?"
- *[justification with no intention of changing behavior]:* "I'm responding to a very important message from my friend Claudia."

The phone example with validation:

- *[acknowledgement of the other person's need or right]:* "Look, Martha, I understand that you need to reply to messages from your friend . . ."
- *[acknowledgement of your own need or right]*: ". . . but I think I also have the right to feel listened to and respected, just as I do with you when you're telling me something that's important for you."
- *[proposed solution]:* "So, if what you're discussing with your friend is really urgent, I'd prefer it if you told me that you can't talk to me right now and let me know when you can give me some quality time."

Other examples:

- "I understand what you're saying, and it makes sense, but I can't do what you're asking me because I'd be risking my job."
- "I understand that you've already made dinner plans for tonight, but I didn't know anything about that until now, and I'm too tired to go."
- "I know you're short on time, but we agreed a week ago that you would give me back my notes, and I really need them now."

If they insist, you can use the broken record technique (explained in the next chapter) while keeping a firm but non-aggressive tone.

* 12 *

LEARNING TO SAY NO

The most important thing I learned after forty was to say NO when it's NO.

– Gabriel García Márquez

When we find it difficult to say no, we tend to invest time, effort, money, and energy on so many things that we end up feeling overwhelmed and stressed. Trying to do everything is the same as not doing anything: It's neither effective nor practical, but rather overwhelming and tremendously frustrating. If you often find yourself thinking, *There aren't enough hours in the day* or realizing you'd like to start doing plenty of things but never find the right moment, and time just passes by, it's time to ask yourself if you're really using your time on what you really want and on what's important to you.

José Luis Sampedro, a renowned Spanish writer, economist, and humanist, once said that "time is not money, because money is worthless. Time is life." If you spend your time on things that are not a priority for you, you end up devoting your life to irrelevant matters; if you spend your time on irrelevant matters, you're basically wasting your life, and when you waste your life, you're also wasting your only chance at being happy.

Time is something that can only be spent. It can never be recovered or returned, because it is finite. It will run out for everyone one day, so everyone should make the commitment to themselves to do everything they can so that, when they take their last breath, they feel it was all worth it. Therefore, what you say yes to and what you say no to are crucial.

Before learning strategies for saying no in an elegant and assertive way, you might find it helpful to reflect on what your priorities in life are and whether you are living in accordance with them.

- Who and what make you feel good about yourself?
- What feels good in your soul and spirit?
- What are your goals? What brings you closer to them and what takes you far from them?
- What would you like to do but never find the time for?
- How much time are you taking away from what is important? How much time are you dedicating to irrelevant things?
- Does the way you organize your time affect your relationships with the people you love?

. . .

Reflecting on the influence the things you say yes or no to can help you be more aware of the importance of those small everyday decisions. Once you're aware of this, you'll automatically understand why it's problematic to make those decisions based on what others will say, on not wanting to look bad, or on not wanting to seem rude. Acting on those motives will never make you feel good if deep down you feel like you're ultimately spending your time doing things that distance you from what is essential to you.

Despite the many reflections that can help you realize the importance of learning how to say no, being able to do it without feeling guilty is a gradual process that requires you to constantly step out of your comfort zone.

You need to keep in mind that, the more accommodating you are, the more difficult it will be for you to get used to saying no, because, on the one hand, the feeling of guilt will be more intense, and, on the other, people who are used to always getting a yes from you will offer great resistance. It's an uphill battle, but the strategies described below will be your best allies.

Saying No with No Further Explanations

One of the most difficult things to do is say no without giving any further explanations. We tend to believe that, if we don't explain why we can't or don't want to do something, we're being rude or impolite to the other person. As I mentioned before, this is doubly mistaken because, first, we assume that not wanting or not being able to do something is not reason enough to refuse, so we completely invalidate our needs or emotions; and second, when we explain ourselves, we open the door for the other person to question us and try to find arguments or alternatives to continue insisting. Keep in mind that, if you don't give an explanation, there is nothing to question because you're basing your decision solely on whether you want to agree to something or not, and that is unquestionable.

We should redefine what it means to say no and to get no for an answer: When you honestly say no, you're conveying that you feel comfortable enough with the person receiving it to be able to sincerely express what you want without the need to embellish it with further justifications. Similarly, when you receive no for an answer, you may appreciate how sincerely the other person is acting and refuse to interpret it as something negative, but rather as a positive sign of honesty.

It's important that you keep in mind that if you've spent your whole life being accommodating to others and saying yes when you actually wanted to say no, you'll need to be very patient with yourself and venture into some trial and error. You'll need to practice tolerance over, and over, and over. Little by little, you'll become familiar with the feeling—at first somewhat uncomfortable but then totally liberating—of saying no until you're able to do it naturally.

To achieve this, apart from implementing the strategies described in this chapter, you may want to learn some phrases to keep up your sleeves and use in situations that catch you completely off guard. Here are some expressions for saying no with no further explanations:

- "I'd rather not. Thank you."
- "I'm sorry, but that's not going to be possible."
- "I'm sorry, but I can't."
- "I don't feel like it today, but thanks for the invitation."
- "Honestly, I just can't."
- "Honestly, I wouldn't feel comfortable doing it."
- "Not today, thank you. Maybe next time."
- "Thanks, but I don't feel like it today."

Thank you + No (+ I'm Sorry) + Pleasantry

This is the most basic assertive strategy for saying no: Thank the person for the proposal or for their trust in you, and then politely decline, adding an optional "I'm sorry," depending on whether you really feel that way or not. Finally, add a polite comment. This last element serves two purposes: to add kindness to your refusal or a good wish for the other person, while subtly and elegantly asking them not to insist.

Nonverbal communication strategy: Speak with a firm and calm tone of voice, and keep eye contact. If you accompany your words with a smile—as long as it's sincere—or a gesture of honest gratitude, despite being a negative response, it will be perceived as a pleasant reply and will be well received by the other person.

Examples:

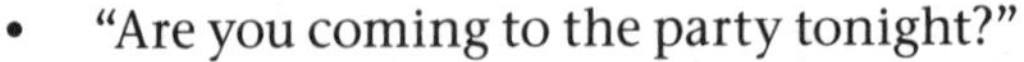

- "Are you coming to the party tonight?"
- "Oh, thanks, but I can't go. I hope you have a great time, though!"

- "I'm cooking dinner tonight at my house. You can't miss it!"
- "Thank you for inviting me, but I have a prior commitment. Sorry. Enjoy yourselves!"

- "I need to finish this report by tomorrow, and I won't make it on time. You're the only one who's qualified enough to help me with this. What e-mail address should I send it to?"
- "Thanks for the compliment, but I can't, I'm sorry. I hope someone else in the department can help you."

- "Can you look after my kids this evening? I've been invited to the movies and I'm dying to see that film!"
- "I really appreciate your trust in me, but I have plans for this evening. I'm sorry. I hope you find someone else available."

Thank You + No + Alternative

This is a variation of the previous formula, but it adds an alternative. This strategy is particularly suitable for those cases in which your refusal could be easily interpreted as a lack of interest or as a way of "putting them off"—for instance, when you're just getting to know someone and want to continue doing so. By refusing their request but offering another plan for a different occasion, you're conveying that you currently can't or don't feel like it, but you do want to spend more time with them later.

Example:
"Are you coming to the party tonight?"

A. "Thanks, but I can't make it tonight. How about we meet up on Sunday?"

B. "I appreciate that you invited me, but I don't really feel like it. Would you like to do something more low-key tomorrow?"

C. "Thank for inviting me, but I'd rather not go. I've been invited to another event tomorrow, though. Would you like to come with me?"

When you're just getting to know a person, this strategy not only helps you show interest in them, despite declining their invitation, but it also lets you gauge whether that person is interested in you or not. If, once you suggest a plan, they reject it without offering an alternative, they might be telling you between the lines that they're not really interested in seeing you anymore. Once you detect this, you should consider giving them space and waiting for them to take the next step.

Asking for an Extension

You might feel pressured to respond to something when you haven't really made up your mind yet. But don't worry! It's okay to ask for some time to consider it! In fact, everyone should do this more often, as it would save us from regretting something or having to tell the other person that we've changed our mind, which is usually more awkward than just saying no from the start.

Therefore, keep in mind the option of asking for an extension to give an answer. Similarly, you should also respect the time that other people might need to make a decision when you ask them to do something.

Examples:

- "We're planning a trip for next month. You're coming, right?"
- "Thanks for inviting me, but I can't say for sure right now. Give me a couple of days and I'll let you know."

- "I have a wedding this weekend. Could you babysit my daughter?"
- "My partner and I were thinking about going away this weekend, but let me talk to them and I'll get back at you."

- "We organized a birthday party for Claudia, and we're each going to chip in $30 for her gift. Are you in?"
- "Let me get organized and I'll confirm tomorrow."

If, after using this technique, they continue to insist, you can use the broken record strategy and even close your posture a little bit by crossing your arms or legs. Instead of keeping your feet and body facing the other person, turn them slightly outward. That conveys that, as far as you're concerned, the conversation is over.

The "Broken Record" Technique

This technique is very effective for saying no, especially if the other person insists, pressures you, or tries to emotionally blackmail you. It consists of repeating as many times as necessary that you don't want or can't do what you're being asked to do, without changing your message or giving any further explanations. The greatest thing about this tactic is that you can multiply its effectiveness by combining it with other techniques.

Example:
Your child insists that you give them money for a video game, but you don't think it's appropriate because they haven't done their homework this week. After their request, you can reply: "I'm not going to give you any money because you haven't done your homework in the last week."

They will probably insist and put on their best puppy eyes, to which you'll respond again, "No, dear. You haven't fulfilled your responsibilities in the last week, so I'm not going to give you any money."

They may insist again, depending on how persistent they are (somewhere between two and maybe even two hundred more times). It's important that you don't raise your voice or use an aggressive tone (even if you're making a huge effort to be patient, stay calm, and refuse to yield.) Simply respond with the same phrase over And over, but always using a calm and firm tone of voice.

Fortunately, most people are not as persistent as a child or a teenager, but they are helpful for training this skill so that it's easier to apply later. Remember: If you can handle a teenager, dealing with anyone else should be a piece of cake.

Examples of a Broken Record Combined with Other Verbal Strategies

- *[request]:* "Mark, are you coming out for a drink tonight for my birthday? Everyone will be there!"
- *[response]:* "Thanks, Chris, but I can't. I have an important meeting tomorrow morning."
- *[insistence]:* "Are you really not coming? Come on! It's just a drink for my birthday! It's a special day!"
- *[broken record]:* "Thanks really, but I can't go. I have an important meeting tomorrow morning."
- *[insistence]:* "Oh, come on! It's just a drink! Don't be such a sourpuss."

If, after using the broken record technique two or three times, they still insist, it's useful to combine it with other formulas such as "thank you + no + pleasantry" to convey that the conversation is over, and that will probably end the insistence. You can say something like this:

- *[broken record + pleasantry]:* "I appreciate the invitation, but I'm not going. I have an important meeting tomorrow. Have a great time."

If the person you're talking to is perceptive, they'll read between the lines and understand that "Have a great time" means "Don't insist, thank you."

Regarding your body language, turn your body and feet slightly outward and stop making eye contact to let the other person know the conversation is over. However, if you're facing a teenage-level insister who's not ready to give up, you'll need to be much more forceful and literal, and firmly ask them not to insist:

- *[persistence]:* "Are you seriously telling me you're not coming?"
- *[broken record + no insistence]:* "Seriously, thanks, but I'm not going. I have an important meeting tomorrow. Don't insist."

The nonverbal communication strategies accompanying the words "don't insist" can be modulated depending on the context and the person you're talking to. In the previous example, where the context is a conversation with a somewhat manipulative co-worker who is very insistent and disrespectful of your decision, it's appropriate to add a serious facial expression and a firm tone of voice to convey forcefulness. However, if this were a different context and there was no manipulative intent from the other party—let's say, where a friend's grandmother insists you stay for lunch and, far from trying to manipulate you, believes that you're declining her invitation out of politeness or because you're shy or don't want to be a burden (you know, the kind of interpretations people sometimes make based on our cultural codes of courtesy)—it may be more appropriate to use body language that softens your "don't insist," such as placing your hands on your chest and slightly bowing your head while closing your eyes for a moment.

With this gesture, despite giving a very clear verbal command, you also convey with your body that you're grateful, thus softening the message while still being explicit. This nonverbal communication cue is useful in all situations where you need to be clear, but not too forceful, given the context or the characteristics of the recipient.

* 13 *

ASSERTIVE STRATEGIES TO RESPOND TO CRITICISM

When you understand that every opinion is a vision loaded with personal history, you will begin to understand that all judgment is a confession.

– Nikola Tesla

Knowing how to take criticism well requires some personal work beforehand so that you're able to recognize other people's opinions for what they are: mere opinions, not the absolute truth.

Everyone's judgment is shaped by their own history, expectations, beliefs, values, personality, preferences, culture, education, and mood. The possible combinations of factors (and many more that may also influence) are endless, so the results that derive from them (i.e., the judgments) are also infinite.

What makes one judgment more valid than another? If you tend to think that other people's judgments are more valid than our own, you condemn yourself to making decisions and evaluating your actions and yourself according to other people's criteria. In short, you sentence yourself to defining your reality based on other people's opinions. But that's a terrible mistake! In addition to burying your own criteria, you condemn yourself to endless frustration, since it's impossible to have everyone's approval. There will always be people who disagree with the way you act, who criticize and disapprove of you, and accepting this as something natural is essential if you want to live in peace.

You should not only be the protagonist, but also the director of your own movie! You can't let others decide for you, as they already have their own lives and make their own decisions. You should let them know this when they try to manipulate you or impose their opinions or behaviors on you. You should be able to tell them, "You're in charge of your own life, and I'm in charge of mine," without any kind of guilt or remorse, just as a basic rule of respect for others and for yourself.

However, that doesn't mean that you shouldn't listen to other people's opinions or criticisms, because they can be great learning and growth opportunities that you should not miss. Quite the contrary: You must learn how to use them to improve and learn from your mistakes. Otherwise, you risk becoming pedantic and stagnant.

If you want to be able to accept criticism in a healthy way, there are two key elements you need to work on: personal judgment and self-confidence. It's essential to know how to evaluate other people's opinions or criticism using and trusting your own judgment. This way, you can analyze their criticisms and extract from them what is useful or refute them without taking them as a personal attack. What's important is that you never accept them without questioning them first nor change your behavior because you value someone else's opinion more than your own without even analyzing it.

This is often a complex process, especially if you're still reinforcing your self-esteem so that it allows you to trust your own judgment and prevents you from feeling undermined by negative external opinions. (If that happened, it would be a helpful sign that you need to work on strengthening it.) Whether or not you have a good self-esteem, it's always difficult to receive criticism that is neither assertive nor constructive, the kind of criticism that lacks empathy or that intends to manipulate you. In these cases, you can respond using the strategies outlined below.

Basic Assertiveness

When faced with criticism, there are three types of responses you should avoid:

- *Aggressive response:* Counterattacking—doing this will likely lead to an argument based on mutual attacks
- *Passive response:* Remaining silent, passively agreeing, or apologizing when you actually think you did nothing wrong
- *Passive-aggressive response:* Agreeing first and then attacking

An assertive way of responding when you're facing non-constructive or manipulative forms of criticism is to openly express that you don't feel comfortable with the way the other person is criticizing you and suggest that they do it constructively.

Examples:

- "Could you say that in a kinder way? I don't feel comfortable with the tone you're using."
- "I don't think it's necessary to say it that way; it makes me feel bad. Could you share your opinions in a more constructive way?"
- "I would like you to use a kinder tone with me."
- "I would appreciate it if you shared your opinions more constructively."

Negative Interrogation

Another possible assertive response is to openly ask the person who criticized you what their reasons are, instead of responding defensively, denying your mistakes, or counterattacking. You can use phrases such as these:

- "What do you think is so negative about [. . .]?"
- "Why do you think [. . .] is wrong?"
- "What do you find inappropriate about [. . .]?"
- "Why would you say [. . .] is not right?"

By replying to attempted attacks or manipulations with an assertive question, you convey three things: that you refuse to engage in aggressive behavior, that you're willing to continue the conversation without belittling yourself, and that you're open to receiving sincere and supported responses. After the other person replies, you can choose whether to accept their criticism as constructive or dismiss it, and you will have also implicitly set a boundary in terms of how you want criticism to be communicated to you next time.

Fog Bank

This technique consists of calmly acknowledging that there may be a bit or a lot of truth in what you've been told, but without agreeing to change your behavior or opinions (as long as they don't violate anyone's rights, of course).

Examples:

- "You have terrible taste in music. Everything you listen to is rubbish."
- "It may not be the best music in the world, but it is what I like."

- "Your phone was stolen on the street? Why would you take it out in public? That's what you get for being so stupid."
- "I may not be the smartest person, but the only one to blame for a theft is the thief."

- "Are you going out dressed like that? It looks like you're thirsty for attention."
- "Well, yes, I want people to look at me."

By not counterattacking, giving unnecessary explanations, or submissively yielding to the manipulation of your critic, they will most likely run out of arguments to continue criticizing you.

The Sandwich Technique

This strategy is useful both for making constructive criticisms and for responding to criticisms in an elegant and effective way.

When You Make a Criticism

The sandwich technique consists of saying something positive first, then introducing the criticism, and then adding another positive aspect. Thus, the critical message is cushioned between two messages of positive acknowledgment, which makes it easier to receive for the other person, as they won't feel attacked and will be more open to corrections.

Example:

- "I loved your presentation. At times your voice sounded a little weak, but you managed to hold the audience's attention from start to finish."

When You're Making a Countercriticism

If you disagree with someone's criticism, rather than responding defensively, you can also use the sandwich technique to reply, especially if the criticism comes from a superior at work or in a similar context. In this case, you'll take a part of the criticism that you think is right and show that you agree with it. Thus, the other person will realize that you're not trying to counterattack and continue listening to your opinion openly and calmly. Then, express your disagreement, and finally choose one of these three positive options:

A. Thank them for their perspective.

B. Suggest a solution.

C. Ask what the other person thinks would be a good solution to the problem.

This way, once again, you'll have two positive elements "cushioning" a negative one, and you'll be able to make a countercriticism both elegantly and eloquently.

Example:

- *[criticism]:* "The report you wrote is too long and gives too many details about the tests that have been made, which is completely unnecessary."

- *[sandwich countercriticism]:* "I agree that the report is a bit too long. However, I do think it's necessary to explain which tests have been carried out and the results that have been obtained in order to justify our conclusions."

  Then follow the countercriticism with one of the three positive options:

  A. *[thanks]:* "In any case, I appreciate your input. I will take it into consideration."

  B. *[suggesting a solution]:* "I think I can summarize the third point a bit more. Do you think that would be enough?"

  C. *[asking the other]:* "Which elements would you eliminate from the report?"

Replying to Mockery and Criticism Disguised as Humor

A Look Is Worth More Than a Thousand Words

When someone mocks or criticizes you using humor, it's common to fall into their trap and laugh (even if you don't really find it funny), downplay it, or simply suppress your feelings because you don't want to seem like a wet blanket or a killjoy.

When you allow someone to say something you find hurtful or upsetting without setting a boundary, you're letting them disrespect you, even if they are using humor to camouflage it. In these cases, as with any other form of disrespect, you need to know how to let that person know that you don't like what they have just said. However, when it comes to setting boundaries for criticism made with jokes and humor, you might feel extra pressure because showing your discontent could not only communicate displeasure but also interrupts the feeling of fun with a reflection you know will create discomfort. However, the use of jokes or humor should not be a free pass to criticize or disrespect anyone. If you are bothered by a comment, whether it was made in jest or not, you need to know how to confront it so that it doesn't happen again.

A simple strategy you can start with is simply responding seriously to the comment: Don't laugh at the joke, and keep eye contact with the other person. Our prefrontal core contains mirror neurons, which specialize in making us empathetic people. When they detect a face expressing an emotion that is completely different from what we're feeling, they send an alarm signal that communicates that something strange is happening. That is exactly what happens when you keep eye contact with the other person without laughing for about three seconds after their comment. Thus, you will activate the necessary areas in their brain so that they themselves realize that what they did was not pleasant for you.

It's possible that this gesture alone prompts the other person to apologize for their behavior. However, if that doesn't happen, you can then implement the following strategy:

Reveal Their Intentions

This strategy consists of openly expressing what you believe to be the person's intention behind their criticism or mockery, making it clear and assertively pointing out the inappropriateness of their behavior.

This is how to do it:

- *Start by repeating the comment:* "When you asked me for the third time if I cut my own hair . . ."
- *Continue by expressing how you feel or what you think:* "I feel like you're trying to ridicule me."
- *Ask a direct question to get confirmation or denial:* "Is that what you're trying to do?"

Once you've followed these steps and asked this last question, the other person may realize that their behavior has been inappropriate and try to apologize. If, on the other hand, you're dealing with a real jerk and their answer to the last question is yes, try not to lose your cool: Carry on with this strategy in a calm but firm tone of voice and ask them, while looking them in the eye, "Interesting, why would you want to do that?"

The answer to this question will be decisive: Either the person will excuse themselves and apologize when faced with this dead end, or, if they give any other type of response that shows they really are a hopeless fool, you can conclude that it's not worth talking to them anymore and you can just walk away, or use one of the strategies for politely telling them to f**k off (which you'll find in the last chapter).

* 14 *

HOW TO SET BOUNDARIES WHEN DEALING WITH MANIPULATORS

The manipulative person sees everyone as a traitor if they don't do what they want.

— ANONYMOUS

"See What You Made Me Do"

People who like playing the victim, narcissists, provocateurs, attention seekers, people who tend to discredit others, opportunists, moralists, blamers, liars, demagogues, hypocrites, abusers, and instigators of all kinds are the type of people who are willing to manipulate us at any cost for their personal gain.

The best thing you can do when you identify one of these people with manipulative behaviors is to avoid having any kind of relationship with them. This is the best way to protect yourself from attacks, emotional and psychological abuse, and toxic relationships. However, sometimes it's not as easy to avoid them because they may be part of your family or work in the same place as you, for instance. In that case, it's better to limit interactions to what is strictly necessary. And, if necessary, you can use the techniques explained in this chapter.

Manipulative people are very skilled at making us feel guilty, afraid, ashamed, or despised when we don't do what they want or when we don't allow them to treat us as they please. That's why when you try setting boundaries with a manipulator, they usually become angry to make you think you did something wrong, feel guilty about it, and end up giving in to their will. But you must stand firm and avoid yielding; this is a battle you cannot afford to lose, and to do so you need to know exactly how to respond to each kind of attempt at manipulation.

If you're a people pleaser or an overly empathetic person, this battle might be more complicated because you're the kind of person who understands the other person's (the manipulator) circumstances, their history or their particular way of being, and end up justifying and tolerating their behavior. But there's a very fine line between understanding and tolerating, and you should be able to identify it so that you avoid crossing it: Being able to understand why someone acts the way they do doesn't mean that you must tolerate their manipulative or abusive behavior.

This usually happens with family or romantic relationships where one person is abusive or manipulative, and the other excuses them because "they had a difficult childhood" or "they're going through a hard time" or "their father beat them when they were little" or "their ex-partner made them very insecure" or "they're very stressed out at work" or whatever. It's one thing to sympathize with someone and another one to avoid holding them responsible for their actions. Remember: Everyone is responsible for their actions, for working on the issues they face, and for seeking professional help, if necessary, regardless of how difficult life has been for them. In other words, just because someone had a difficult childhood—or was even the victim of abuse or manipulation—that doesn't justify them harming others. Accepting our past and working on the emotional wounds it caused, without burdening others for it, is part of our responsibility as adults.

It's essential to keep this in mind so you don't end up being anyone's emotional punching bag nor making someone else your own. If you need a punching bag, there are mental health specialists—such as myself—who are capable of taking those "blows" without being hurt, because we aren't personally connected to the abuser and know how to put emotional distance between ourselves and each case. In therapy, you can learn to use tools that help you manage your emotions better, modify your maladaptive behaviors, and heal your emotional wounds, and only the therapist is responsible for guiding you through this process. It's not the mother or the partner or the lover or the brother or the cousin or the friend who are responsible for "changing" the manipulator's behavior or way of thinking. The only person who's responsible for changing is the manipulator themselves, with the help of their therapist.

Most of the people who suffer from having a relationship with a manipulative family member, romantic partner, or friend had the intention of "helping" them from the beginning of the relationship, until they became trapped in their tentacles, and now they are the ones who need help. If you feel you have sympathized with someone like this and believe that they need help, the best thing we can do for them and for ourselves is to suggest that they seek professional help and keep as much distance as possible.

However, what if you can't distance yourself from the manipulator as much as you'd want? Far from counterattacking, making excuses, or ignoring their manipulative behavior, the strategies outlined below will help you learn to act assertively but firmly, and thus clearly establish your boundaries.

Minimize Exposure

If you have no choice but to maintain contact with these kinds of people, it's best to limit your exposure to them as much as possible, convey concise messages, and try to use a polite and calm but firm tone of voice. Try to remain as calm as possible, because, if you let the other person know they have the power to influence your mood, you'll only be reinforcing their behavior. Therefore, do your best not to become upset or aggressive, but also don't be submissive. Just be firm and don't fall for their manipulations. When you act in a way that's unexpected for them, they may become angry or want to manipulate you even more. At this point, it's useful to use the fog bank technique or to offer validation along with the broken record technique (don't do it more than three times in a row) before withdrawing from the conversation.

Examples:

- *[manipulation]:* "I don't want you to go on that trip alone. You should listen to me. I'm your mother!"

- *[validation + firm opinion]:* "I understand that you don't think it's a good idea, but I'm an adult now and I've decided that I will do it."
- *[insistence + manipulation]:* "Don't you care that your mother is worried about you?"
- *[validation + broken record]:* "I understand your position, but I've made up my mind."
- *[persistence + manipulation]:* "After everything I've done for you . . . you don't care about my suffering."
- *[validation + broken record]:* "I understand that you're worried about me traveling alone, but the decision has been made."

Body Language

One of the key points when dealing with this kind of person is to command respect and confidence. In this regard, your body language is key, since you can't try to command respect while your body language conveys fear or submission. Use the basic formula for assertive nonverbal communication but subtly modulate your tone of voice and your gaze.

Your tone of voice needs to be a little firmer and, if possible, deeper. This will reinforce the level of firmness by half a point, which is necessary in these circumstances.

On the other hand, the message you want to convey through eye contact is: "I'm here, I'm clear about my needs and rights, and I won't allow you to violate them, just as I won't violate yours." To convey this with your gaze, it might help you to repeat this message mentally, over and over, while keeping eye contact with the other person, as if you were trying to convey what you're thinking through telepathy. This exercise is very useful when you need to externalize emotions or qualities (such as confidence, respectability, credibility, etc.) with your gaze in order to reinforce your verbal messages. You'll continue using this kind of nonverbal communication with most of the other strategies outlined below.

Use Imperatives

If someone violates your rights, disrespects you, or intentionally crosses your boundaries, it's best to communicate very directly that you won't allow them to cross that line. In these cases, it's most effective to use clear and straightforward imperatives or messages such as "I will not allow / consent to / tolerate this."

If you tend to act submissively, you may find this difficult and may even become somewhat aggressive when you start speaking so directly, but you should view it as a strategy for emotional self-defense, which sometimes is the only way to prevent others from hurting you.

- "Don't interrupt me! I haven't finished speaking."
- "Please don't yell at me."

- "Don't insinuate that I'm crazy ever again."
- "I won't let you insult me."
- "Stop doing that! You're being violent to me."
- "Don't try to blackmail me with that."
- "Don't ever treat me like that again."
- "I won't tolerate you blaming me for this."
- "I won't allow you to disrespect me."

Point Out the Other Person's Behavior

This strategy is helpful when someone's communication style is aggressive or if they try to manipulate you. It consists of two actions: First, explicitly describe the other person's behavior to make it clear to them. Second, warn them that, if they don't change, you'll end the conversation—thus, setting the boundary.

Examples:

- "You just disrespected me, and I won't tolerate it. I will end this conversation if there is no respect."
- "You're yelling at me. I think it's better if we talk at some other time."

- "You're talking to me very aggressively. If you don't change your tone, we'll have to continue talking some other time."
- "You're trying to make me feel guilty for something that isn't my responsibility. Let's talk again when you've had time to calmly reflect on this."

Silence

Silence can express more than a thousand words. You've probably met nosy people who ask totally inappropriate and uncomfortable questions full of ulterior motives, and, if they catch you off guard, you might not have known how to respond. The best way to respond to these situations is with silence, but not with a shy silence accompanied by an evasive look or by pretending you didn't hear them. It should be an imposing, conscious silence, along with a steady gaze that lasts for about three seconds. That silent, direct gaze conveys the message clearly, without the need to make it explicit. Most likely, with this response, the person will realize the inappropriateness of their question and apologize, excuse themselves, or change the subject.

Replying with Another Question

If, after that silence, the other person doesn't acknowledge their intrusion, then you can add another question, such as

"Why are you asking me that?" or "Why are you interested in that?" By responding with another question, the other person will realize that you don't want to answer their intrusive question and will probably withdraw it or change the subject.

"Thanks, but I'll not dignify that with an answer"

After your silence and your question, the other person might still not realize (or not *want* to realize) that you don't want to answer. If they reply with something such as "I just wanted to know" or "because I care about you," then you'll need to be more explicit and respond with an "*I* message" and optionally, if you think it's appropriate, thank them for their concern.

Examples:

- "I appreciate your concern, but I don't want to talk about it."
- "Thanks for asking, but for now I'd rather keep that private."
- "I'd rather not talk about it now, but thank you for caring."
- "I would prefer it if you didn't ask me about that."
- "I don't feel comfortable talking about that subject."
- "It's better if we don't bring that up."

Replying to Sanctimonious or Authoritarian People

If someone tells you that you should act a certain way or imposes their way of doing things as if it were the only correct one, you can start by using the strategy of pointing out their behavior. If that doesn't work, you can respond to their moralizing with another question that makes explicit what they're implying, so they have to confirm or deny whether that's what they mean.

Example:

- *[moralizing]:* "You should have thought about that before you got married."
- *[pointing out the other person's behavior]:* "I think you're judging me harshly without putting yourself in my shoes."
- *[insistent moralizing]:* "I'm not judging you. I'm just saying you should have realized this before. Now it's too late!"
- *[making explicit what's implicit]:* "Are you saying that, because I didn't realize this before, I now have no right to rectify it and deserve to be stuck in this situation for the rest of my life?"

Replying to Know-It-Alls

Many people confuse freedom of speech with having the right to comment on the lives, bodies, or decisions of others when they haven't been asked for their opinion. In cases like these, it's quite useful to have a few assertive and elegant phrases memorized that make it clear you don't want their opinion.

There's a wide range of issues and topics that people might have an opinion on, so, depending on the topic and how it affects you emotionally, you may choose more or less forceful responses.

Examples:

- "I understand you've shared your point of view because you want to help me, and I appreciate that, but this is something I want to decide / do on my own."
- "Thank you for sharing your opinion, but I've already made up my mind. Thank you for respecting it."
- "I know your comment wasn't meant to be hurtful, but this is an issue that makes me feel very insecure, and I'd prefer it if you didn't comment on it unless I ask you to."

- "I understand you want to give me your point of view, but I would rather not receive any more opinions on this subject."
- "Thank you for your opinion, but this matter concerns only me, and I appreciate your respect for that."
- "I feel uncomfortable receiving comments on the subject, so I would appreciate it if you stopped commenting on it."
- "I appreciate hearing different opinions and points of view, but I prefer to receive them when I ask for them."
- "This is a very personal matter, and I would prefer that you refrain from commenting on it."
- "My body [or anything related to it] is none of your business, and I ask that you respect that."
- "I like my body [or any aspect of it] just the way it is, thank you."
- "I don't like people commenting on my body [or anything related to it], thank you."
- "I think it's disrespectful to comment on other people's bodies [or any other aspect of them]. Please don't do it again. Thank you."

Any of these can be good responses to unsolicited comments. Depending on who makes the comment, what it is about, and what their intentions are, one response may be more appropriate than other.

Replying to "Forked Tongues" (Gossips)

There's always someone who spreads gossip and rumors that cause suffering to those involved in them. If you don't want to participate in this kind of malicious chatter, you can respond to people with forked tongues by applying the triple filter Socrates proposed for dealing with this type of situation. The story goes like this:

> One of Socrates's disciples came to him excitedly to tell him something bad he'd heard about someone else. The disciple said: "Do you know what I've been told about your friend?"
>
> Socrates remained silent for a few seconds before answering: "Wait a minute. Before you tell me, I want you to answer three questions so I can decide if your message is worth listening to."
>
> "Three questions?"
>
> "Yes. These are three filters. The first is the filter of truth: Are you absolutely sure that what you're about to tell me is true?"
>
> "No," said the disciple. "It's just something I heard."

"Okay, so you're not sure it's true. Now comes the second question, the filter of goodness. Is what you're going to tell me about my friend something good?"

"No," said the disciple, "quite the opposite."

"So, you want to tell me something bad about my friend even if you're not entirely sure it's true."

The disciple nodded, admitting Socrates was right.

"Let me ask you one last question, which is the filter of usefulness: Will that information you want to tell me about my friend be useful to me?"

"I don't think so," the disciple admitted again.

"So, if what you want to say isn't true, isn't good, and isn't useful to me, why would you want to share it with me? What is your intention?"

Truth, goodness, and usefulness were the three filters Socrates used to respond to this kind of situation. Although it's been centuries, his triple filter remains an excellent premise for determining both what we choose to hear and what we choose to say.

Replying to Guilt Trippers

Someone can make you feel guilty only if your own internal judge agrees with them. In Chapter 6, we discussed guilt and presented a simple framework that lets you identify whether you're judging yourself fairly (or in a healthy way) or unfairly (in an unhealthy way).

You can follow that same outline when someone blames you to ask yourself whether you're really responsible for what you've been accused of. Thus, your inner judge will decide whether to feel responsible for what happened or not. If you conclude that you're neither guilty nor responsible, you can use the following suggestions to reply to those who seek to blame you.

Make Them Justify Their Answer and Open the Debate

- "Why exactly do you think I'm responsible for this?"
- "How have I disrespected you or violated your rights to make me feel guilty for how you feel?"
- "Why do you think it's my responsibility to . . . ?"

Point Out Their Manipulation

- "I think you're making me feel guilty because I didn't do what you wanted me to do. Is that right?"
- "When you say that [. . .], I think you're trying to make me feel guilty so that I feel bad and do what you want me to do."
- "I feel like you're trying to make me responsible for [. . .]. Is that what you're trying to do?"

- "What you mean by this is that I'm to blame for [. . .]?"

Defend Your Behavior and End the Conversation

- "I've made my decision based on my own needs, without attacking or hurting anyone. If this bothers you, maybe we should reconsider whether your definition of well-being and mine are compatible."
- "I can understand that you feel upset because things didn't turn out the way you wanted, but I can't accept you holding me responsible for how you feel."
- "I have the right to make decisions about my life and my body. I'm sorry if that upsets you, but it's not my responsibility."
- "I haven't violated any of your rights or disrespected you, so I'm sorry you're upset, but don't hold me responsible for it."

* **15** *

POLITE WAYS OF TELLING PEOPLE TO F**K OFF

*Time puts everyone in their place. But, if you keep telling people to f**k off, you'll get ahead.*

– Fernando Fernán Gómez

Water and Oil

You've tried everything. You've expressed yourself assertively. You've communicated your needs to the other person and told them what you like and what you don't like. You've been flexible whenever you could be. You even put yourself in their shoes to see the world through their mental map. But even so, the relationship isn't working! What should you do then?

It happens often that people simply aren't compatible, and that doesn't mean that any of them are bad, manipulators, or psychopaths. We just don't fit together. It's like water and oil; no matter how much we want to mix them and make the mixture perfect and homogeneous, it's never going to happen. Is anyone to blame? Is there something wrong with the water? Is there something wrong with the oil? No! Water and oil just don't mix. Period.

The same thing happens with people. Some of us are like water and others are like oil, and there is nothing wrong with either. We're simply incompatible! The mistake we make is that, in most problematic situations, we tend to look for someone to blame. It seems that we need to burden someone else with the responsibility for things not turning out as we expected in order to feel at ease, instead of just accepting that, in many cases, no one is guilty or innocent and there are no good or bad people, no heroes or villains.

When a relationship doesn't work, it's common to get stuck on the idea that we can't break it off unless there is a "bad guy," someone who treats us badly, doesn't care for us and is toxic, narcissistic, or selfish. But . . . what if there isn't? What if you're with a beautiful and nice person, but you still suffer? What if their boundaries and yours are incompatible? What if their needs are incompatible with what you can offer them and vice versa? What if you argue constantly because you don't speak the same language and have very different outlooks on life?

All of this causes pain. The fact is that you can love someone deeply and yet be incompatible with them because, unfortunately, love alone isn't enough to support healthy relationships. When you finally understand that you can love someone deeply but be incompatible with them, you begin to accept that distancing yourself from them might be the best way to love both yourself and them.

Making the decision of walking away, "not because I don't love you, but because, despite loving you, this hurts," is a very difficult step to take, but staying in that relationship will probably lead you to a spiral of indefinite suffering, and you'll exhaust your energy and emotional health in an effort to make it work. And that can be even more difficult.

In that case, rather than telling the person to f**k off, you should talk to them calmly and lovingly (never angrily or with the intention of arguing) to explain the reasons behind your decision to end the relationship and agree together—especially in the case of romantic relationships—how the separation will take place so that it hurts as little as possible for both. This requires, on the one hand, having a healthy self-esteem that allows you to prioritize your own well-being, regardless of how much you love the other person. On the other hand, you need to have emotional maturity, strength, and responsibility.

It's not easy.

This is what is called an amicable, healthy, respectful, and careful breakup with another person (that is also respectful of ourselves).

However, there are times when suffering is caused deliberately and maliciously by manipulators, abusers and narcissists of all kinds. In these cases, you shouldn't think twice about distancing yourself from them—and you're already doing so every time you respond to their attacks with respect and assertiveness, but sometimes that's not enough. Sometimes you have to tell people to f**k off without remorse.

"F**k off! Now!"

One day of 1998, actor and writer Fernando Fernán Gómez was presenting one of his most famous books in Madrid. While reporters from the national television news team were interviewing the author, something epic happened that all Spaniards will remember until the end of time. An admirer approached Fernán Gómez at a completely inopportune moment and asked him insistently to sign his book. The actor, running out of patience, suddenly replied: "Just no! Don't you understand? Don't you? If you think I have a bad temper, well, guess what? I do! And a very bad one at that!" The fan, with an expression of disbelief and indignation, replied: "I used to admire you. But not anymore!" To that, Fernán Gomez responded, "Leave me alone. Stop admiring me. I don't need your admiration. F**k off! Now!"

While it's true that some people find it easier to tell those who annoy, insult, or upset them to f**k off, most of us are in the opposite extreme: We put up with the unbearable because we don't want to offend the person making us miserable, or worse, make them think that we want them to stop making us miserable. We'd rather keep quiet and endure until our dignity is completely buried, which is not far off.

If you're unable to stand up for yourself, you'll never be able to stand up for others. You need to be very clear that you cannot allow anyone to violate your rights, disrespect you, restrict your freedom, or try to manipulate you. In other words, putting yourself in your place means committing yourself to doing what needs to be done to protect yourself emotionally, even if that means disapproving of other people or distancing yourself from them.

We are able to deal with the disapproval of others, but never with our own. Paradoxically, we tend to act as if getting external approval was more important than getting our own approval, and thus try to please people who treat us with contempt, even if that means betraying ourselves. We are disloyal to, treacherous, and dishonest with ourselves just to please others, and then wonder why we have low self-esteem. How can you love someone who treats you that way?

If you don't protect yourself, take care of yourself, and cultivate a good relationship with yourself, you'll spend your life searching outside yourself for something you can only find within. And it's not because there aren't people willing to give it to you, but because, even if they do, you'll never feel that it's enough if you fail to receive it from yourself. It's an endless search, an insatiable struggle, trying to fill a void that only you can fill. Without self-love, no external love will be enough for you.

Loving yourself means caring for yourself, respecting yourself, and protecting yourself from evil, and that often means saying "F**k it!" F**k appearances, f**k what others will say, f**k diplomacy, f**k shame, f**k cowardice, f**k blackmail, f**k other people's expectations, f**k discretion, f**k good manners, f**k impositions, f**k manipulations, f**k subtleties, and f**k shitty people.

Indeed, f**k it!

Very (and Not So) Polite Ways of Telling People to F**k Off

Telling someone to f**k off is a very personal thing. Everyone has to find their own style for doing it. Some people prefer being elegant, whereas others use sarcasm or bluntness or maybe even do it directly without any room for error. Depending on your personality, the moment, and the person you're going to tell off, you can use different styles. What's undeniable is that the more resources you have, the more skilled you'll be in this subtle art.

There is one particularly important thing to keep in mind when telling someone to f**k off, and that is that telling them to f**k off usually means putting an end to communication or to the relationship with that person. It doesn't mean "I dislike what you said" or "I disagree with your point of view" (previous chapters have been devoted to expressing that kind of opinions). What it means is "I will no longer tolerate your manipulation or disrespect, and this is where we part ways." But you must be consistent with the message; in other words, you cannot tell someone to f**k off and then continue listening to them or stay in a relationship with them as if nothing had happened, because then you would lose all credibility—and your dignity, for that matter.

When you tell someone to f**k off, you must always be consistent with that verbal message and accompany it with adequate nonverbal communication strategies and other actions. Thus, you need to focus on three moments: the moment right before you deliver the message, the moment in which you deliver the message, and the moment right after delivering it.

Right before delivering the message: When the other person makes a hurtful, manipulative, or intrusive comment, you'll start by communicating nonverbally, keeping eye contact with the person you're talking to for one to three seconds without saying a word. Remember that your gaze is the most powerful form of nonverbal communication that you have, because the eyes say what the mouth doesn't. So you can convey a message with your eyes without saying a word. The trick is to keep in mind what you'd like to tell the other person while looking at them directly in the eyes. ("You're a jerk!" "You're manipulative," "Why don't you go to hell?" or whatever comes to your mind at the moment.) The silent space of three seconds has a triple function: first, to convey a message of disapproval; second, to allow you to assess whether the message you have thought of is exactly what you want to say, depending on the context and after weighing the possible consequences; and third, in case you want to say what you want in a different way, to give you enough time to determine the most appropriate way to do it.

When you deliver your message, the more calmly you can tell someone to f**k off, the more control you'll show you have over the situation and over your emotions, and the more elegant you'll seem. To do it, you need to speak clearly at a medium voice (not too loud but not too soft) and look the other person in the eye. Regarding your posture, you don't need to keep an open posture as you would in assertive communication, because you have already used all the assertiveness you can muster and have reached a point where, rather than being assertive, what matters to you is protecting yourself from verbal attacks and manipulation. So, if it comes naturally to you to cross your arms at chest level or to put your hands to your hips, do it. Remember that this is not an attack, but emotional self-defense.

After delivering your message, you'll need to make a physical or verbal retreat. A physical retreat would consist of leaving the place where the other person is. It's only a matter of grabbing your belongings, turning around, and with great dignity, leaving the place without looking back. Thus, you're conveying the message that not only have you claimed that you won't tolerate the other person's manipulation / abuse, but you're also denying them the opportunity to continue doing so.

When it's not possible to withdraw physically, you'll have to do it verbally. That means ending the conversation as follows: After communicating your message, stop keeping eye contact with the other person (since eye contact calls for an answer), but don't look down, for that would convey submission, fear, or nervousness. What you need is to point your entire body (including your face) far from where the person is, thus confirming nonverbally that you're no longer paying attention to them, and start doing something different. If you have nothing to do, you can pick up your phone to make a call or reply to a message, grab a notebook and start writing, put on your headphones and listen to music, fold a napkin into origami. . . . It doesn't matter what you do, as long as it's something that doesn't involve talking to the other person.

As for verbal messages, it's best to keep them short and to the point, without too many explanations, since the way the other person treats you is explanation enough. Then make your retreat immediately after delivering the message—withdraw physically, whenever possible, but at least verbally.

Below you'll find some ideas for replying to typical manipulative phrases (which can be replaced by any other

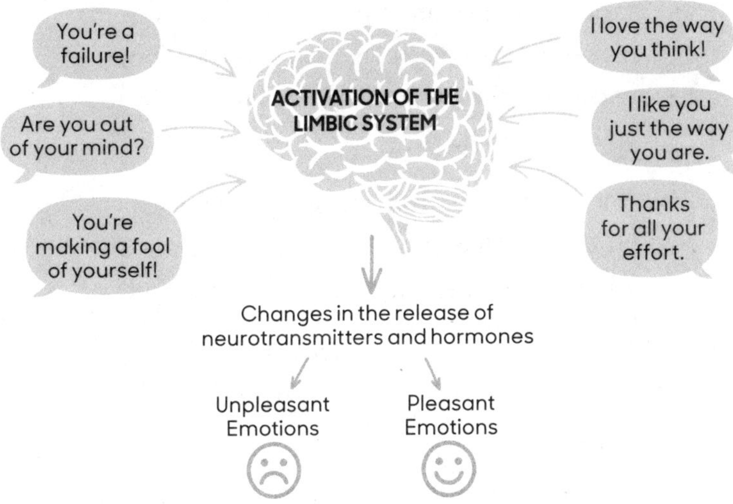

manipulative phrase), although I highly recommend you let your imagination run wild and come up with some replies of your own.

Replying to Manipulative Phrases that Assign Blame

Examples:
"See what you made me do." "I did it for you." "This is all your fault."

Responses:

- "You're trying to manipulate me, but that's not going to work on me anymore" [+ retreat].
- "You're trying to make me feel guilty for something that isn't my responsibility. Unbelievable!" [+ retreat].

- "You're trying to manipulate me by making me feel guilty / fearful, which says a lot about you as a person. I have nothing more to say to you" [+ retreat].
- "I learned a long time ago how to spot this kind of manipulation, and I won't tolerate it anymore. We're done talking!" [+ retreat].
- "I'm tired of you trying to manipulate me, and I won't allow it anymore" [+ retreat].

Replying to Manipulative Phrases that Attempt to Justify Lies

Examples:
"I didn't lie, I just omitted information." "I didn't tell you because I was trying to protect you."

Responses:

- "Just because something isn't a lie doesn't mean it's not deceitful" [+ retreat].
- "Trying to cover up your lies doesn't make them true, nor does it excuse you for breaking my trust" [+ retreat].
- "It's ridiculous that you try to justify your lies with that argument. I'm sorry, but I don't want to have a relationship with someone who lies to me" [+ retreat].

- "The blatant way in which you try to manipulate me leaves me speechless and makes me very disappointed" [+ retreat].
- "The only thing I want from people who lie to me is to be as far from them as possible" [+ retreat].

Replying to Gaslighting

Examples:
"You're crazy!" "You don't know what you're saying." "You're paranoid!"

Responses:

- "You invalidated my emotions and disrespected me, and I won't allow it. This conversation is over!" [+ retreat].
- "I won't tolerate you insulting me or treating me like I'm crazy / stupid / paranoid / dramatic. . . . We're done talking" [+ retreat].
- "I'm not falling for your manipulative tricks anymore" [+ retreat].
- "I can't find any qualities in you that make up for the way you treat me" [+ retreat].
- "I was hoping for a mature and rational conversation, but I see that's not going to happen" [+ retreat].

Replying to Emotional Blackmail

Examples:
"If you loved me, you would sacrifice yourself for me." "After all I've done for you . . ."

Responses:

- "I didn't expect you to try to emotionally blackmail me this way. I'm sorry, but I won't take the bait" [+ retreat].
- "Trying to emotionally blackmail me says a lot about the kind of person you are" [+ retreat].
- "People usually do what they do because they want to do it, without expecting anything in return. But you're using that to get something from me, and that's outright manipulation. I'm sorry, but things don't work that way with me" [+ retreat].
- "If you're going to rub it in my face every time you do something for me, I'd rather you didn't do anything" [+ retreat].
- "My concept of love doesn't involve suffering. I'm sorry, but if we can't agree on this, then this relationship should end" [+ retreat].

Replying to Unsolicited Opinions

Examples:
"You've gained / lost weight!" "You looked better with long hair." "You should have a stricter schedule with your baby."

Responses:

- "Honestly, I don't appreciate what you just said."
- "That's an interesting observation, but I think it's inappropriate to share it unless you're asked."
- "Would you mind giving me your opinion on this matter only if I ask you? Thank you."
- "If I didn't ask for your opinion on this, it's precisely because I don't want to hear it."
- "Next time I want to know your opinion, I'll ask you. For now, I'm not interested in it."

Other Sarcastic, Witty, and Funny Ways to Tell Someone to F**k Off

- "Here's your nose back. It was all up in my business."
- "Did you smell that? I think it's what you just said."

- "Sorry if I can't meet your expectations, but my priority is only to meet my own."
- "When you're a simple person, you run the uncomfortable risk of being taken for a fool."
- "I hope the rest of your day is as pleasant as you are."
- "Sorry, but I have no adequate answer for someone with your level of maturity."
- "We can all say stupid things at some point in our lives, but some people abuse that privilege."
- "You've got a bit of crap stuck between your teeth."
- "Talking with your mouth full is impolite, but talking with an empty head is worse."
- "It seems you were picked before you were ripe."
- "Please find somewhere else to exist."
- [An artistic version] Draw a huge circle and say, "This is how much I care about the birth rate of Asian ants [or whatever absurd thing comes to your mind] and this [draw a dot] is how much I care about your opinion of me."

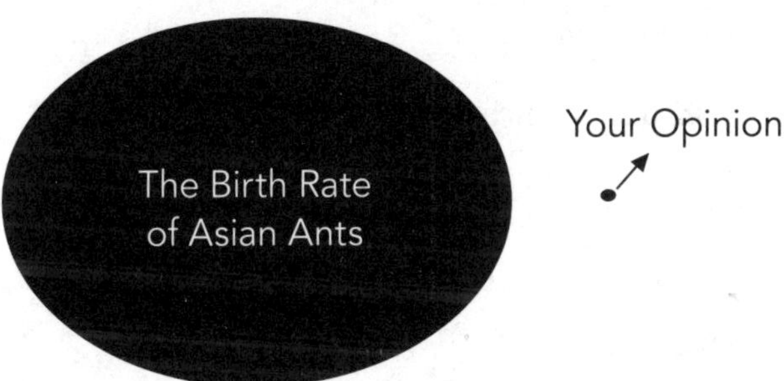

The litany of ways to tell someone to f**k off could fill hundreds of pages, but it's more fun to use your own creativity and ingenuity to come up with original ways to ask people to get lost, to go to hell, to go tuck themselves in, to spare you the pleasure of their company, to build themselves a bridge and get over it, or to let them know that their absence is required, thus enhancing your talent, wit, and subtlety in this refined—yet grotesque—art of telling someone to f**k off, and finding your own way of doing it.

Below you'll find some old-timey insults that can help you form original expressions for telling people to f**k off. Use them as you please and let your imagination run wild.

- *abydocomist:* a liar who brags about their lies
- *backfriend:* a seeming friend who is secretly an enemy
- *balatron:* a buffoon, a contemptible fellow
- *bespawler:* a slobbering person who spits when they talk
- *blunderbuss:* a dumb, blundering fellow

- *bobolyne:* a fool
- *churl:* a rude, mean-spirited person
- *cumberground:* someone who is useless
- *dandiprat:* a contemptible or insignificant person
- *dunderhead:* a stupid person
- *faitour:* a cheat or impostor
- *foozler:* a bumbler or clumsy person
- *fopdoodle:* an insignificant or foolish person
- *fribble:* an idler and a good-for-nothing
- *frippet:* a showy, frivolous young person
- *gobemouche:* a very gullible person
- *gollumpus:* a clumsy person
- *grinagog:* a foolish person who smiles constantly
- *grumbletonian:* a constant complainer
- *lubberwort:* a lazy, stupid person
- *makebate:* someone who incites conflict and unnecessary arguments
- *mediocrist:* an average person of no distinction and without remarkable talent

- *mumpsimus:* a person who stubbornly clings to false beliefs
- *muck-spout:* someone who talks and swears a lot
- *nigmenog:* a very silly person
- *poltroon:* an utter coward
- *quisby:* someone who shirks from work
- *ragabash:* a disorganized or grubby person
- *rakefire:* a guest who outstays their welcome
- *rattlecap:* an unsteady, volatile person
- *roiderbanks:* someone who lives beyond their means
- *rumbumptious:* a pompous person
- *saddle-goose:* an imbecile
- *scobberlotcher:* a lazy person
- *smelfungus:* a hypercritical person
- *sneaksby:* a mean-spirited fellow; a sneaking coward
- *snollygoster:* a shrewd, unprincipled person
- *snoutband:* someone who constantly interrupts others, usually to contradict them
- *sorner:* someone who lives off other people

- *stingbum:* a cheap, selfish person
- *stymphalist:* someone who smells terrible
- *wandought:* a weak and ineffectual person
- *whangdoodle:* someone who loudly and angrily complains about things
- *wrinkler:* someone who's prone to lying
- *zoilist:* an overly critical nitpicker

There are many more you might want to add to create unique and original ways to tell someone to f**k off, but of all of them—past, present and future—the one that is most relieving, the one that is most freeing and leaves no room for misunderstanding or confusion is, without a doubt, a simple, clear, and resounding

ABOUT THE TRANSLATOR

Ariadna Molinari Tato has translated for Penguin Random House, Planeta, and other publishers in Mexico and Latin America. She specializes in fiction, YA literature, and health. She has translated dozens of books into Spanish, including works by Hilary Mantel, Joyce Carol Oates, Shirley Jackson, George R.R. Martin, and Cecelia Ahern. Additionally, she teaches translation at the National Autonomous University of Mexico.

ABOUT THE AUTHOR

Alba Cardalda is clinical psychologist, neuropsychologist, and specialist in cognitive-behavioral therapy as well as brief and strategic therapy. For more than 12 years, she has helped thousands of people feel good about themselves and their relationships. Her best-selling books, *How to Tell People to F**k Off Politely* and *How to Stop Being Your Own Worst Enemy*, have sold hundreds of thousands of copies in Spanish and will be translated and published in more than 35 countries.

Website: **albacardalda.com**

Instagram: **@albacardalda.psicologa**

TikTok: **@albacardalda.psicologa**

Hay House Titles of Related Interest

YOU CAN HEAL YOUR LIFE, the movie,
starring Louise Hay & Friends
(available as an online streaming video)
www.hayhouse.com/louise-movie

THE SHIFT, the movie,
starring Dr. Wayne W. Dyer
(available as an online streaming video)
www.hayhouse.com/the-shift-movie

• • •

Conscious Communications: Your Step-by-Step Guide to Harnessing the Power of Your Words to Change Your Mind, Your Choices, and Your Life, by Mary Shores

The Let Them Theory: A Life-Changing Tool That Millions of People Can't Stop Talking About, by Mel Robbins

Protect Your Peace: Nine Unapologetic Principles for Thriving in a Chaotic World, by Trent Shelton

Self Help: This Is Your Chance to Change Your Life, by Gabrielle Bernstein

All of the above are available at your local bookstore, or may be ordered by contacting Hay House (see next page).

• • •

We hope you enjoyed this Hay House book. If you'd like to receive our online catalog featuring additional information on Hay House books and products, or if you'd like to find out more about the Hay Foundation, please contact:

Hay House LLC, P.O. Box 5100, Carlsbad, CA 92018-5100
(760) 431-7695 or (800) 654-5126
www.hayhouse.com® • www.hayfoundation.org

Published in Australia by:
Hay House Australia Publishing Pty Ltd
18/36 Ralph St., Alexandria NSW 2015
Phone: +61 (02) 9669 4299
www.hayhouse.com.au

Published in the United Kingdom by:
Hay House UK Ltd
1st Floor, Crawford Corner,
91–93 Baker Street, London W1U 6QQ
Phone: +44 (0)20 3927 7290
www.hayhouse.co.uk

Published in India by:
Hay House Publishers (India) Pvt Ltd
Muskaan Complex, Plot No. 3,
B-2, Vasant Kunj, New Delhi 110 070
Phone: +91 11 41761620
www.hayhouse.co.in